ADULT RELIGIOUS EDUCATION

THE 20th CENTURY CHALLENGE   BY LEON McKENZIE

Second Printing—1977
Third Printing—1979

ISBN 0-89622-024-9

Retail price: $5.95
Bulk order discounts offered on purchases of 10 or more copies.

This book, *Creative Learning for Adults* by the same author, and *The Church As Reflecting Community* by Loretta Girzaitis comprise the Adult Educator's Library, available as a unit from the publisher.

Meet the Author

Leon McKenzie is Hospital Education Coordinator for Indiana University Hospitals and Associate Professor of Adult Education, Indiana University. He completed the doctoral degree in adult education at Indiana University as a Lilly Fellow and a Bergevin Fellow. He is author of *Designs for Progress, Process Catechetics,* and *Christian Education in the 70's.* He was editor (with John McKinley) of *The Diagnostic Procedure in Adult Education* and is editor and author of *Participation Training: A System for Adult Education.*

He has taught a variety of graduate courses in adult education at Indiana University. He has also designed educational games for Twenty-Third Publications and has written Twenty-Third's popular bestseller, *Creative Learning for Adults.*

Preface

The twentieth century is a century of change. Call it what you will—flux, evolution, development, discontinuity, or transition—change is the prevailing constant of our era. Change has touched all aspects of life: social structures, economics, employment, politics, religion. And the pace of change has been great. A person who is 50 years old today has witnessed a degree of change roughly equivalent to the amount of change experienced by ten generations of his pre-twentieth century ancestors.

The enduring fact of twentieth century change is significant for adult education. In many areas of life the present-day adult has been prepared educationally to live in another world: the world of ten to forty years ago. Obsolescence chases us all—and at a gallop. Perhaps this is more proper to adult religious education than to any other kind of adult education. Adult education, then, is a **challenge** more than anything else, a summons issued to adult educators by history, a gauntlet cast at the feet of those who help adults learn.

The collection of essays comprising this book is for the front-line practitioners of adult education. The essays are essentially introductory in nature, but hopefully some of the ideas expressed in the following pages will be of benefit to seasoned veterans in the field of adult education. This volume has been prepared to assist adult educators, in some small way, to deal with the challenge imposed on them by present-day events.

I owe much to Neil Kluepfel of Twenty-Third Publications for hectoring me, in a friendly way, into writing the book. To Dr. John McKinley, Department Chairman of Adult Education at Indiana University, I extend my thanks for sharing his expertise with me on innumerable occasions and for exemplifying what it means to be a gentleman and a scholar.

I wish to thank my associates, colleagues, and students at Indiana University for stimulating me by their questions and kindness. Virginia Heckman prepared the typescript in her own

Dr. Paul Bergevin

inimitable professional style and made valuable suggestions regarding clarity of expression; she was ably assisted by Florence Bilikha. To both of these ladies I say, "Thanks."

While others have been associated with what is good in the book, they are not to be blamed for its deficiencies; I take full credit for what is lacking.

Finally, I dedicate this volume to Dr. Paul Bergevin, Professor Emeritus of Adult Education at Indiana University. He has been my professor, confidant, mentor, and friend. He has been a constant source of encouragement to me. I shall never be able to repay his kindness, but I do wish to make public note of it.

Leon McKenzie
Hospital Education Coordinator
Indiana University Hospital
Assistant Professor of Adult Education
Indiana University

Table of Contents

1. What Is Adult Religious Education?

Educational practitioners, by and large, have a passion for the practical. Many teachers of adults and/or administrators of adult programs are ever in search of instruments, approaches, tools, texts, devices, plans, gimmicks, tricks, fads, and strategies that will assist them in their work. This is not to be faulted. What can be faulted, however, is the neglect of principles and theories that sometimes accompanies the pursuit of the practical.

The late Kurt Lewin once remarked that nothing is more practical than theory. Paul Bergevin, Professor Emeritus of Adult Education at Indiana University, indicated to me on several occasions that the greatest failure of teachers of adults is their indifference to principles and theories. He stated that many people want to construct a building by first erecting the roof, and that these people were not fond of laying a foundation at any stage of the construction.

Without a theoretical foundation, the most promising of practicalities in adult education are nearly worthless. A theoretical foundation provides a rationale—a consistent and systematic framework—for teaching and learning activities. A teacher without educational principles is like a ship without a rudder; educational activities guided by such a teacher usually turn out to be directionless and aimless: an exercise in collective nervous activity.

The minimal requirement for adult educators is that they know what adult education is. The very least to be expected of religious educators of adults is that they be able to express what adult religious education is. A chemistry teacher who is unable to explain what the word "chemistry" means would not provoke a surfeit of confidence among his students. An adult educator who cannot make some intelligent response to the question "What is adult education?" may cause raised eyebrows and lowered expectations among adult learners.

In this initial essay I wish to address the question "What is adult religious education?" But before this question can be answered, it will be necessary to define adult education. This is so because adult **religious** education is a potential part of adult education pure and simple. This essay, then, will not be of the "how to" variety; the chapter will focus eventually on "why."

Adult Education: Three Meanings

There is a degree of confusion and ambiguity attached to the words "adult education." This is because "adult education" may

Without a theoretical foundation, the most promising of practicalities in adult education are nearly worthless.

be viewed in three basic senses. Adult education may refer to: 1) a field of professional study and research, 2) a body of knowledge about the adult learner, the teaching-learning process, program planning, and so forth, and 3) the teaching-learning process as it relates to adult learners. In the professional field of adult education research is undertaken and a body of knowledge is generated. This body of knowledge is applied, ideally, in the teaching-learning situation.

Without prejudice to adult education as a professional field or as a body of knowledge, when the term "adult education" is used in the remainder of this chapter it will refer to the teaching-learning process.

Adult Education: A Definition

Within the past decade an international group of professional adult educators pooled their efforts and stated a working definition of adult education. The definition appears in *The Exeter Papers.*[1]

In *The Exeter Papers* adult education is viewed as:

1. a process . . .

2. involving persons who no longer attend school on a regular and full-time basis (unless fulltime programs are designed especially for adults) . . .

3. the process is constituted by sequential and organized activities . . .

4. learners have the conscious intention of bringing about changes . . .

5. the changes are changes in information, knowledge, understanding, skills, appreciation and attitudes . . .

6. sometimes learners have the conscious intention of identifying and solving personal and community problems . . .

The process of adult education, according to *The Exeter Papers,* may take place in any of five broad categories:

1. Remedial education: fundamental or literacy education, education that is necessary as a prerequisite for other kinds of learning.

2. Education for vocational, technical, and professional competence: education that prepares the learner for a job or helps a person keep abreast of developments in a professional field.

3. Education for health, welfare, and family living: education that includes topics relating to health, family consumerism, child-care, and so forth.

[1] Liveright, A.A., and Haygood, Noreen (eds.), *The Exeter Papers,* Center for the Study of Liberal Education for Adults, Boston: Boston University, 1968, pp. 8-10.

4. Education for civic, political, and community competence: education that includes topics relating to government, community development, political affairs, voting, and so forth.

5. Education for self-fullfillment: education that includes *liberal* or leisure time offerings; education in music, the arts, theater, literature, and so forth. This kind of learning is "learning for the sake of learning" and not learning to achieve aims included in the other four categories.

A Critique

Although the definition of adult education presented in *The Exeter Papers* discloses some important features about adult education, the definition is not beyond criticism.

First of all, the description of an adult as a person who no longer attends school on a full-time basis is too narrow. Non-attendance at school on a full-time basis is a criterion that produces some striking contradictions when applied to concrete cases. For example: John quit school when he was sixteen and now drives a truck for a living. According to the definition, John is an adult. Bob, on the other hand, is a junior in college and is 20 years old. According to the criterion, he is not an adult.

Secondly, no mention is made in the definition of the educational agent or teacher who directs the educational process.

Thirdly, the goals of the adult educational process as stated in the definition are immediate. Long-term goals are not mentioned. In this the definition appears to lack sophistication and discrimination.

Finally, in categorizing forms of adult education it seems that adult religious education has not been adequately treated or reckoned with—an amazing phenomenon given the fact that adult religious education constitutes a large part of the total adult education enterprise.

Adult Education: Another Definition

No definition of adult education is perfect; every definition will be open to justifiable criticism. This truth applies to the following definition just as much as it does to others.

> **Adult education is a formally structured process in which an educational agent enables adults to actualize their potentialities to the end that they become more fully liberated as individuals and more fully prepared to participate in bettering the life of the communities to which they belong.**

Several elements of the definition require further elaboration.

No definition of adult education is perfect; every definition will be open to justifiable criticism.

A. Formally structured process . . .

Adults learn by living; they learn randomly and experientially. Anyone who has been around for a sufficient number of years is likely to assimilate some knowledge and develop some human powers. The words "formally structured process" in the definition indicate that the teaching-learning events follow an orderly system or sequence, and that the teaching and learning is planned rather than indiscriminate.

B. Educational agent . . .

The educational agent is a person or persons responsible for fulfilling various managerial roles in the educational process. Several role functions are subsumed under the rubric of educational agent: a) assessing the adult learner's needs or interests, b) planning the educational process, c) implementing the process, and c) evaluating the results of the process.

C. Enables . . .

The educational agent is an enabler, a facilitator, a guide. The educational agent desires autonomous behavior of the adult learners and avoids dominating or manipulating the learners.

D. Adults . . .

An adult is understood to be a person who is socially perceived as an adult: one who has undergone some kind of rite of passage from adolescence such as obtaining a full-time job, graduating from secondary school, getting married, being inducted into military service, establishing an independent domicile, etc.

E. Actualize potentialities . . .

Ideally, the educational process assists adults to develop unrealized capacities and unfulfilled talents. These talents may be in the area of vocational education, literacy education, professional education, religious education, and so forth.

F. Liberated as individuals . . .

The goal of education is liberation. Hegel wrote that freedom is the ultimate purpose toward which the processes of history have continually aimed. He insisted that freedom is the final aim of God's intent for the world.[2]

To be human, in the richest sense of the word, means to grow in all dimensions of personality and be a self-transcending animal. But before growth or self-transcendence is possible, a

[2] Hegel, G.W.F., *Reason in History,* New York: Bobbs-Merrill, 1953, p. 25.

person must be free to grow. Adult education ideally liberates persons **for** self-transcending activities and **from** whatever stifles human growth.

G. Prepared to participate . . .

It is not enough that individuals are liberated and that the growth of individuals is fostered. Indeed, it is questionable whether any individual can become more human, if he does not enter into dialogue and collaboration with others. Man is a self-transcending animal; he is also a social animal. The social aspect of human nature is such that self-transcendence is not possible without social interrelationship. Self-transcendence and individual growth do not occur in a social vacuum.

H. Bettering the communities . . .

John Dewey observed the linkage among the words "community," "communication," and "common."[3] Persons live in community by virtue of the fact that they share things in common, and they share things in common because of communication. The definition proposes that adults participate with one another to better community life precisely so that individuals may continue to grow and develop. The development of individual competencies is a means to the end of achieving a richer community life; the development of a richer community life is a means to the end of facilitating further individual growth. The relationship is reciprocal.

Adult Religious Education: Its Nature

Adult religious education is a part of adult education as defined above. This is to say, adult education pure and simple encompasses a wide variety of educational types: vocational education, professional education, community education, literacy education, health education, religious education, and a host of others forms.

What complicates understanding the meaning of adult religious education is that religious education may be **religious** either in terms of content or by reason of intent.

When the content of education concerns theology, liturgy, scripture, and doctrine, adult religious education may be defined as follows:

Adult religious education is a formally structured process in which an educational agent enables adults to actualize their **religious** potentialities to the end that they become more fully liberated as individuals and more fully prepared to participate in the life of the communities to which they belong.

[3] Dewey, John, *Democracy and Education,* New York: The Free Press, 1966, p. 4.

What complicates understanding the meaning of adult religious education is that religious education may be *religious* **either in terms of content or by reason of intent.**

The term "religious" in the definition distinguishes adult religious education from adult education pure and simple.

Adult religious education may be religious by reason of the educational agent's intent. The intent of the educational agent is to serve the needs of the learners and this intent is based on religious affirmations and convictions. The educational agent may be teaching the poor how to use food stamps more effectively (something that has little to do with the concept of religion in its most obvious sense) and yet he could be engaged in religious education because of his religious intent to help the poor.

The definition of adult religious education would then be formulated as follows:

Adult religious education is a formally structured process in which an educational agent, because of his religious convictions, enables adults to actualize their potentialities to the end that they become more fully liberated as individuals and more fully prepared to participate in bettering the life of the communities to which they belong.

It is true, of course, that both content and intent may correspond. A person may help others learn religious concepts because of his religious beliefs.

What I am trying to express by offering two slightly different definitions of adult religious education is that adult religious education may address itself either to the so-called profane needs of people or to the so-called sacred needs of people. There are not two orders of reality; the sacred and the profane. There is one order of reality as we perceive it: the human. Adult religious educators cannot neglect the secular needs of people with the excuse that "after all, we are **religious** educators and, therefore, should not concern ourselves with worldly needs."

Conclusion

As a consequence of being able to respond to the question "What is adult religious education?" the teacher of adults will not necessarily become a more effective teacher. But at least he will become a teacher who can rationally justify his existence as a teacher. He will at least have some anchorage in theoretical principle and will understand his teaching activity in terms of far-reaching normative values. And this, it is maintained, is good. It will prevent the teacher from appraising himself merely as a trained automation who is going through complex motions for some immediate "pay off."

There is nothing wrong with a "bag of tricks" in education. But a bag of tricks will not get any teacher very far. The "bag of tricks" approach to education will work only when the teacher also carries a bag of principles. Just as form follows function in architecture, principle precedes procedure in education. A teacher must know when, how, where, and which tricks to use; more importantly he must know why.

Just as form follows function in architecture, principle precedes procedure in education.

2. The Mud Below: An Opportunity

A number of years ago a movie was produced about stone-age peoples living in a corner of the earth bypassed by civilization. The title of the film was *The Sky Above, The Mud Below.* The stark beauty of peaceful skies above the tribal settlement was contrasted with the subsistence level needs of the people. I often think of the film when I reflect on the content of adult education programs in parishes and local churches.

Tendentious is a big word. It means "marked by a tendency to a particular point of view." Without being hypercritical or negative, I suspect that most adult programs in parishes and local churches are tendentious: there is a tendency to focus on theological abstractions, scriptural studies, and liturgical speculations. There is a tendency to emphasize the spiritual works of mercy over the corporal works of mercy; there is a tendency to talk about the sky above and to neglect the mud below.

In the previous chapter I suggested that adult education may be religious either by virtue of the **content** of courses or by virtue of the **intent** of those who implement the courses. A course on the Gospel of Matthew would be religious by virtue of its content; a course on homemaking could be religious by virtue of a religious response to real human needs. In this chapter I wish to outline some general areas of adult education that can be sponsored by the churches. While the content of these suggested courses is not religiously oriented, the courses can be religious in that they may represent a response of a caring community to mundane needs of people.

. . . . Most adult programs in parish and local churches are tendentious: there is a tendency to focus on theological abstractions, scriptural studies, and liturgical speculations. There is a tendency to emphasize the spiritual works of mercy over the corporal works of mercy . . . .

TEN POSSIBLE COURSES

1. Education for basic literacy

Many adults, particularly the poor and disadvantaged, entertain no hope of personal development because they are unable to read or write. They are handicapped in a very real sense and are unable to follow basic procedures when seeking employment. The illiterate person is not able to read the "help wanted" advertisements in the newspapers; he is unable to fill out application forms for jobs; he is often ashamed to admit to prospective employers that he is illiterate. We may be entering what some cultural commentators call the "postliterate era," but education for basic literacy is still supremely important for many adults.

2. Education for the G.E.D.

Some people drop out of high school and subsequently find it difficult to find a job because they lack a diploma. Other dropouts soon realize that the path to economic improvement and social mobility is blocked because they have not completed high school. But their problem is not insurmountable. They can be prepared to take tests leading to the General Education Diploma. Assistance can be offered them in tutorial programs or in special classes for groups.

3. Education for child care

Many parents, especially among the poor, are not prepared to care for their children. Some parents lack the basic knowledge of sanitary conditions, proper diet for children, and childhood illnesses. They are unable to cope with child care problems which are considered elementary by the majority of the population. They need help and this help can be supplied in the context of an educational program funded and staffed by a cluster of local churches or parishes.

4. Health education

Many people, and not only the poor, are unacquainted with some common measures of preventive medicine. They do not know what to do in case of health emergencies. Much educational work needs to be done in the area of mental health and in the area of venereal diseases. Health education courses could be carried on by volunteer physicians, medical students, and nurses with a minimum of expense and effort. It may be possible for churches to collaborate with local hospitals in this educational venture.

5. Legal education

There is a great deal of truth in the saying of Oliver Goldsmith that laws grind the poor while rich men rule the law. Poor people generally do not know the law. For that matter, large numbers of middle-income people have never been afforded the opportunity to become familiar with the law. They do not know where to turn when they are in legal trouble; they become easily enmeshed in legal intricacies. Even a rudimentary knowledge of legal matters would benefit many people and preserve them from much bewilderment and frustration.

6. Consumer education

Education for consumerism is greatly needed, particularly in times when economic difficulties are great. Many people know next to nothing about credit buying, budgeting, interest rates, insurance, or the economic assistance that is provided by governmental agencies in times of emergency. Consumer education will help people conserve their economic resources and make them more astute when it comes to spending these resources.

7. Political education

In a democratic society the power of the ballot is ideally the means of initiating change in the social system. When groups of adults gather political cohesion they can elect lawmakers sympathetic to their needs. But before people can work "within the system," they must know something about the system. Adults cannot usually operate as political animals on the basis of what they learned in a junior high school civics class. They must discover how they can organize politically and use political leverage to effect change.

A political education course sponsored by a parish or local church could pass on information regarding voter registration and serve as a center for the discussion of political issues. Knowledge of political tactics would be helpful to multitudes of people who feel the pressures of powerlessness. This is not to suggest that churches align themselves with specific candidates or political parties; it is to indicate that education for civic and political participation is necessary.

8. Specific skills training

In at least one former residence of religious, the kitchen has been used as a training center for a culinary arts course. The people who are trained in the center will eventually find employment as chefs, cooks, and waitresses. Churches could offer a wide selection of training courses in specific skills with the assistance of volunteer instructors: auto mechanics, cosmetology, metal work, drafting, home repair, etc. These kinds of courses entail some expense, but are highly valuable for meeting the real earth-bound needs of many adults.

9. Communications skills training

Communications training encompasses all forms of communications that take place among people. Individuals can be helped to express themselves more articulately; groups can be trained to work together as units. People can be trained to listen more effectively, to interpret incoming messages with greater skill, and to handle ideas with a greater facility. A communications training course could be profitable for members of church committees and councils.

10. Family life education

Many adults find it difficult to live together in the family unit. Socio-cultural events in the present time can fracture families and produce a lack of cohesion among members of a family. A family life course would concentrate on strengthening the bonds of family unity. The course could be conducted by psychologists or home economists on a volunteer basis.

PROGRAM ORGANIZATION: TWO DIRECTIONS

Educational courses that meet the mundane needs of adults should meet two criteria: 1) the effort should have a broad ecumenical support base and 2) the courses should be directed to non-churchgoing adults as well as to members of the sponsoring churches.

One of the major reasons why religious education for adults is not generally organized ecumenically is due to the different commitments of people to specific theological viewpoints. A number of programs now in operation help people from different Christian communities understand one another's commitments and viewpoints. But it is not usual to find a cluster of churches supporting a single educational program for adults in a given area of civic community. The religious content of a course will vary theologically depending on whether the course is sponsored by a Methodist, Presbyterian, Baptist, or Roman Catholic church. The absence of pooled resources among different churches concerning religious content courses is, to a degree, understandable.

Courses of study that are religious by virtue of intent, and programs that are designed to meet the "secular" needs of adults, may be jointly sponsored and supported by different Christian bodies with little difficulty. While a Roman Catholic pastor might have qualms about directing his parishioners to a Unitarian Church for a course on the morality of birth control, he can have no reasonable qualms about encouraging his parishioners to attend a course on consumerism at the Unitarian Church—particularly if the course is sponsored collaboratively by the ministerial alliance and sponsored by a cluster of area churches of different denominations.

Courses that are designed to meet the secular needs of adults should be promoted not only among the members of the churches that sponsor the courses but also among the non-churchgoing population. Courses that are religious by intent are directed toward meeting **human** secular needs; these courses are provided as service courses to those who stand in some kind of educational need.

PROGRAM ORGANIZATION: PROBLEMS

Two kinds of problems may be anticipated in organizing the type of program outlined above: 1) priests and ministers may have trouble selling the idea to members of their churches, 2) members of the non-churchgoing population may suspect that something is "fishy" about attending courses sponsored by churches even when the content of the courses have nothing to do with the study of religious ideas. The first problem is an administrative problem; the second problem is a promotional one. Both of the problems are essentially human relations problems.

Members of various churches will not always see how courses devoid of religious content can be authentically religious. Courses about the bible, church history, or theology may qualify for their moral and financial support; courses about adult literacy or preventive health measures, some will think, should be implemented somewhere else and not in a religious setting. The Church, it will be argued, should stick to its doctrinal arena and leave secular knowledge to secular institutions.

If resistance to the idea of sponsoring education that is religious by intent is great, there may be a need to provide people with a course of study on the nature of the Christian stance toward "neighbor." At all costs, some attempt must be made to justify a secular program in terms of the gospels and to respond to objections to the program. Ministers, priests, and directors of religious education may initiate a program by administrative fiat and without popular support. But such a tactic would not augur well for the proposed program. Innovative programming in education should always have some measure of popular support. If the support is not present, it should be generated.

In promoting courses of the type just mentioned it must be made clear that the courses are provided as a service to everyone in the area or town, and that church membership is not a precondition for attendance. Announcements of the courses can be made in the church bulletins of the sponsoring churches and from the pulpits. Announcements should also be made elsewhere: in the shops on Main Street, at places of work, to voluntary associations in the neighborhood, and to community service agencies. Some community service agencies may also be asked if they wish to co-sponsor particular courses, e.g., the Red Cross may welcome the chance to co-sponsor with the churches a course on preventive medicine.

AN OPPORTUNITY FOR SERVICE

A few years ago I listened to an interesting sermon given by a minister at an ecumenical celebration. He told the parable of the lighthouse. To the best of my ability I shall repeat the parable here.

Once upon a time, along the rocky shores of an eastcoast state, many ships foundered on the jagged rocks outside of a particular town. A leader in the town convinced the people to construct a lighthouse to warn ships of possible dangers. The lighthouse was built and operated by the townspeople. For many years the townspeople flashed out warnings to unsuspecting ships and, thereby, saved many people from disaster.

After forty years or so, the lighthouse won the acclaim of all New England. The townspeople became very proud of their lighthouse, so proud in fact, that they began holding meetings at the lighthouse to discuss the nature of the lighthouse, the history of the lighthouse, the goals of the lighthouse, and so forth. The townspeople became so engrossed in these meetings that soon they began to neglect the operation of the lighthouse. Thereupon many ships began to rush to destruction on the rocks. For all practical purposes, it was as if there were no lighthouse there at all.

The moral: unless they are careful, members of churches can transform their lighthouse into clubhouses.

Many adults today are in need of educational services addressed to their immediate earthly needs. These needs cannot be met unless a legion of social institutions, including the churches, get into the business of human need. It seems to me that a fantastic human service can be provided by religious institutions in this country, if only educational programs in the churches are oriented in directions other than the theological.

In advising that churches embark on educational ventures that meet secular needs, it must be noted I am **not** arguing that current religious content courses be dismantled. Quite obviously there is a place in educational programming in a parish or local church for courses of study that concern religious themes. But there is also a place in the educational programming of parishes and local churches for courses that respond to the mundane needs of adults Such a place exists, if for no other reason, because many human beings are in need of such a service.

In advising that churches embark on educational ventures that meet secular needs, it must be noted that I am *not* **arguing that current religious content oourses be dismantled.**

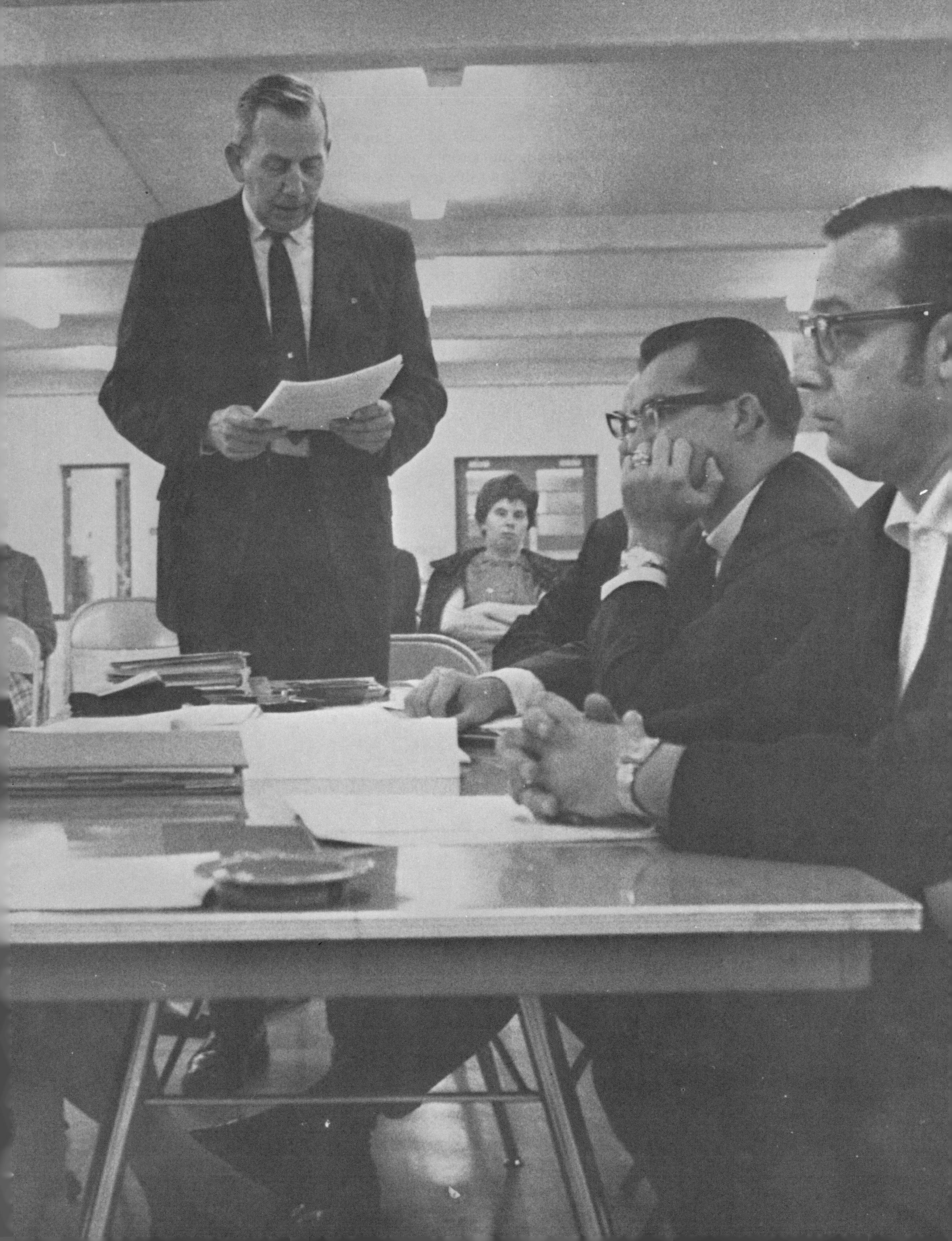

3. Key Concepts for Adult Educators

It was pointed out in the previous chapter that many teachers of adults are eager to learn "practical" things about adult education but are reluctant to engage in speculation about principles. This concern for practice is an overarching concern; regard for theory is minimal.

But ask any teacher of adults if he should possess a coherent system of values that guide activities in the educational situation and he will probably say yes. No doubt the words "theory," "philosophy," and "principle" are perceived as mysterious and formidable. While at the same time, it is generally recognized that guiding principles are a necessary part of the equipment of the adult educator.

Theory, philosophy, and speculation about abstract principles can be boring and can appear to have little bearing on the "real" world. Some philosophers can become so abstruse that they put their audiences to sleep. But this need not be. Philosophical principles can be stated simply without being simplistic. Adult educators can be introduced to theory in such a way that they can immediately grasp the relevance of principles to practice.

One of the books that expresses some principles of adult educational philosophy in a succinct and matter-of-fact fashion is Paul Bergevin's *A Philosophy for Adult Education*.[1] For twenty-five years Dr. Bergevin was director of the Bureau of Studies in Adult Education, Indiana University. He is now Professor Emeritus of Adult Education. Bergevin's philosophy, as stated in the aforementioned book, is particularly relevant to what is called "volunteer" adult education: that form of adult education in which adults participate for no immediate, palpable gain. "Volunteer" adult education may be contrasted, for example, with the kind of adult education that takes place in business and industry. In the latter type, learners take part in educational enterprises to gain a raise in salary or a promotion. "Volunteer" adult education, the kind that takes place in church settings, must be supported by general principles of philosophy just as all other kinds of adult education. Bergevin has enunciated, I suggest, several principles that apply directly to adult religious education.

---

[1] Bergevin, Paul, *A Philosophy for Adult Education*, New York: Seabury Press, 1967.

In this chapter I wish to extract some of the key concepts of Bergevin's philosophy and state some guidelines for teachers of adults. Instead of lifting whole paragraphs from *A Philosophy for Adult Education,* I shall attempt to capture the general flavor of Bergevin's thought. It should be underscored that my characterizations of his philosophy may not be adequate or precise (although every effort has been made to be exact). If there are any weaknesses in this chapter, they should be attributed to me and not to Bergevin. How accurately I portray Bergevin's philosophy must be measured by those who read both this chapter and *A Philosophy for Adult Education.*

AFFIRMATION OF THE ADULT AS LEARNER

Bergevin affirms the adult as learner. The adult can learn. This simple principle is based on research and on the experience of professional adult educators. The principle belies the old piece of folklore that "you can't teach old dogs new tricks." This confidence in the adult as a learner runs throughout the entire fabric of Bergevin's philosophy.

If the teacher of adults assumes that adults are somehow "retarded" in their capacity to learn, he will fail to challenge them sufficiently.

Whether a teacher of adults believes that adults can learn has extremely important consequences. If the teacher of adults assumes that adults are somehow "retarded" in their capacity to learn, he will fail to challenge them sufficiently. When the teacher of adults gives credence to the proposition that old dogs can't be taught new tricks, the total learning environment will be affected adversely. The teacher will easily fall prey to despair in difficult times. He will enter the teaching-learning situation with expectations of failure and his expectations will usually be met. The idea of self-fulfilling prophecy applies to adult education.

The teacher of adults, therefore, must affirm the abilities of adults to learn.

PERSONALISM

In his philosophy of adult education Bergevin is always conscious of the dignity of the adult learner and the respect that is due to adults as persons. In philosophical terminology this would be called a **personalist** orientation. People are more important than things; people deserve respect and consideration; the needs of individuals and their communities are to be acknowledged and given priority over the desires and needs of the teacher.

Again, respect for persons may seem to be a simple principle. But it does happen with greater frequency than we like to admit that people are sometimes treated as things in educational programs. All too often teachers of adults are so task-oriented, so enthusiastic about getting something done, that they neglect to be people-oriented. Adults are sometimes treated in the same way a domineering teacher deals with fourth graders. The accumulated wisdom and the rich experiences of adults are discounted.

The teacher of adults must appreciate the worth of adult learners and must allow this appreciation to govern his relationships with adult learners.

FREEDOM

The concept of freedom is emphasized in Bergevin's philosophy. This concept is understood in three ways: 1) adults must enter the educational situation freely; 2) adults must be permitted to exercise their freedom in the learning situation; 3) one of the great purposes of adult education is the growth of responsible freedom in the learners.

It may be possible to constrain adults to attend an educational offering, but it is unlikely they will be coerced to learn. When adults freely choose to participate in a program, they will make an investment of self in the program and will work to accomplish the educational goals. If they are pressured into attending an educational offering, this self investment will not be made and learning will not take place. "Volunteer" adult education must truly be volunteer; adults must be motivated to participate in education because of the intrinsic worth of the program and because the program meets their needs and interests.

Once adults have presented themselves for learning, every effort should be made to involve them in the decision-making process regarding the teaching-learning process. This means that the teacher of adults must be flexible enough to permit the learners to adjust the goals of the course and to accommodate the teaching-learning plan to their needs. While it is not always possible to involve the adult learners in decision-making in "non-volunteer" learning, they must be involved as fully as possible in "volunteer" adult education.

Growth in individual freedom is encouraged and fostered by allowing adults to exercise freedom in the teaching-learning situation. A person develops responsible freedom by acting freely and responsibly. If this principle is foremost in the mind of the teacher of adults, if growth in responsible freedom is seen in the larger scheme of things as a goal of adult education, the teacher's attitudes and behavior will undergo a change for the good.

Those who are responsible for adult education in the parish should not resort to subtle "arm twisting" in order to increase enrollments in adult programs.

Teachers of adults should invite adult learners to collaborate in making decisions about the teaching-learning situation.

Growth in learner freedom as a goal of adult education should be the prevailing idea of the teacher of adults.

INSTITUTIONAL AND INDIVIDUAL NEEDS

. . . . Bergevin stresses that existing institutions are the most effective bases for adult education.

At a time when institutions of all kinds are caught in a cannonade of criticism, Bergevin stresses that existing institutions are the most effective bases for adult education. Man is a social animal and has established various institutions and organizations to meet the requirements of the social dimension of his nature. These institutions and organizations can be utilized for adult education. But this sometimes poses difficult problems.

Should institutional needs take precedence over individual educational needs? Should individual needs and interests or institutional goals be the foundation for the development of educational programs? Stated more specifically, should the content of educational programs be determined by the bishop of the diocese and the pastor or by those who will take part in the programs?

Realistically the question is not of the "either-or" variety according to Bergevin. Representatives of institutions should **collaborate** with learners in determining the goals of educational programs. The pastor, for example, has every right to suggest that certain topics be treated in the parish program of adult education. He may see some institutional/parish goals not recognized by the learners. The learners also have every right to suggest topics for their learning activities; if they provide no suggestions for the development of programs, they will probably be exposed to a program of institutional indoctrination and not to an educational program, strictly speaking.

I must sadly conclude that a large number of religious education programs for adults are founded on institutional goals rather than individual needs.

On the basis of my previous experience and discussions with hundreds of adult educators from a variety of churches, I must sadly conclude that a large number of religious education programs for adults are founded more on institutional goals than individual needs. Work must be undertaken to achieve a balance in the future. Individual needs and interests must be assessed to a greater degree than they are today. Religious education programs for adults must meet both institutional goals and individual needs.

MATURITY

Adult education ideally assists the adult learner to become mature. As understood by Bergevin, maturity means the development of the individual toward **wholeness** in order to achieve constructive spiritual, vocational, physical, political, and cultural goals.

The concept of maturity connotes essentially the notion of **continuing** lifelong growth. The mature person is not content to rest on past laurels; he is not satisfied with a stagnant personality. The mature person is one who realizes his limitations and attempts to grow beyond the present boundaries of his personality.

Just as an acorn is necessary for the growth of an oak, some degree of maturity is required before an adult is prompted to participate in education. It takes a mature person to understand that the search for wholeness is a lifelong quest, an odyssey that is never quite finished. This initial degree of maturity that serves as a motivator for adult learners "arrives" when a person finally recognizes that life is not merely to be lived passively in bovine complacency but is, instead, a project. Life is ours not to have and to hold, but to develop. Like the talents in the New Testament, life is not to be wrapped in a napkin and buried; life is to be used productively and constructively.

While some degree of maturity is necessary at the beginning of the adult's participation in educational programs, a fuller degree of maturity is developed through education. Thus, one of the major goals of adult education is the development of maturity on the part of the learners.

The implication of this for the teacher of adults is obvious: if you wish adult learners to grow in maturity, you must treat adult learners as mature persons. People learn responsible freedom by practice; they are able to become more mature through the practice of mature behaviors in the teaching-learning situation. In a very real sense the process of adult education **is** the product.

THE CIVILIZING PROCESS

A central idea in Bergevin's philosophy—perhaps **the** central idea—is the notion of the civilizing process. The total social environment teaches people to relate to one another with understanding, dignity, and love. If the total social environment accomplishes this, the environment can be called a civilizing process—a process that stimulates rationality in individuals and institutions. Because of the civilizing process the evolutionary movement of human society is directed toward humanization. Someone once observed that the missing link between apes and civilized man is **us:** a thought that expresses the meaning of the civilizing process.

But the civilizing process does not occur automatically and without human intervention. Social processes can become barbarizing as well as civilizing. Social processes influence people,

Someone once observed that the missing link between apes and civilized man is *us:* a thought that expresses the meaning of the civilizing process.

but in a reciprocal manner people influence social processes. As Bergevin notes, the civilizing process advances in proportion to the number and quality of the adults who play an active part in the process.

People must learn how to contribute to the civilizing process. And by people I mean children as well as adults, but especially adults. The power to influence society, after all, resides in the adult population. Childhood education may assist to develop the civilizing process twenty years from now, but adult education may assist to make a better tomorrow.

One of the ultimate goals of adult education, then, is the development of the civilizing process and the development of a civilized product: a "place" where persons understand, respect, and love one another.

CONCLUSION

Many of Bergevin's ideas can be expressed in theological terminology. The idea of the civilizing process, for example, can be understood as *redemptive* **process. The redemptive process moves ahead in proportion to the number and quality of religiously committed people who take an active part in the process.**

Many of Bergevin's ideas can be expressed in theological terminology. The idea of the civilizing process, for example, can be understood as **redemptive** process. The redemptive process moves ahead in proportion to the number and quality of religiously committed people who take an active part in the process.

It is not surprising that Bergevin's **philosophy** of adult education is amenable to translation into a **theology** of adult education. While Bergevin has been influenced in the development of his thought by a host of other philosophers (Aristotle, Dewey, Lindeman, Hegel, Whitehead, and Overstreet to mention a few), I find that he has entered dialogue, perhaps, more often with Grundtvig (a nineteenth-century Danish bishop) and St. Paul.

The ideas of Bergevin deserve a greater currency among adult religious educators. Perhaps this brief chapter has served to introduce the philosophy of Paul Bergevin to adult religious educators who are yet unfamiliar with his work. Hopefully teachers of adults will embark on their journeys in adult education with more than a nodding acquaintance with the very practical, yet very profound, insights of Paul Bergevin.

4. Andragogy: A New Idea for New Times

Any introduction to the foundations of adult education would not be complete without an examination of the concept of andragogy as developed by Malcolm Knowles. Knowles is perhaps the best known adult educator in the country. He has enjoyed a distinguished career in adult education and is presently one of the most active professionals in the field. For many years he was chairman of the adult education department at Boston University. Currently he is professor of adult education at North Carolina State University.

Dr. Malcolm Knowles

Discussions of the concept of andragogy can be found in two of the books authored by Knowles: *The Modern Practice of Adult Education*[1] and *The Adult Learner: A Neglected Species.*[2] Simply stated andragogy is the art and science of helping adults learn; pedagogy is the art and science of helping children learn. Andragogical approaches are based on what we know about adults as learners; pedagogical procedures are based on traditional assumptions about childhood learning.

PEDAGOGY

Pedagogy comes from two Greek words: PAID (child) and AGOGUS (leader of). We deal with children educationally at least partly because of the assumptions we make about them. Children are assumed to be dependent rather than independent. It is assumed further that their life experience is slight and unnoteworthy, that they "ought" to learn certain things in the present that will be applied in the future, and that their learning should be subject-centered rather than problem-centered. Whether these assumptions are correct is another question. The

---

[1]Knowles, Malcolm *The Modern Practice of Adult Education,* New York: Association Press, 1971.

[2]Knowles, Malcolm, *The Adult Learner: A Neglected Species,* Houston: Gulf Publishing Co., 1973.

fact is that these assumptions are made and, thus, influence the manner in which children are treated educationally. Pedagogy has come to refer to that type of education that is transmissive and appropriative. That is, the teacher transmits information to the child and the child appropriates this information to himself.

Pedagogical norms, which are typically unstated, govern what happens in the education of children. The teacher is regarded as an authority figure; the children are viewed as unassertive and acquiescent. Educational planning is the responsibility of the teacher alone. The teacher determines, unilaterally, what the children need educationally. Educational goals are formulated by the teacher in splendid isolation from the children. Classroom tasks are defined in terms of how the teacher is to present the subject matter. The teacher fills out the report card and evaluates how well the children have appropriated the subject matter.

The teacher determines, unilaterally, what the children need educationally. Educational goals are formulated by the teacher in splendid isolation from the children.

ANDRAGOGY

Andragogy comes from two Greek words: ANER (man, in the sense of a grownup person) and AGOGUS (leader of). We should deal with adults andragogically because of certain qualities that are characteristic of most adults. Adults are independent instead of dependent; they possess a self-concept of self-directedness and are not as easily pushed around as children. In fact, many adults will not tolerate being pushed around at all. Their life experience may be great and enriched. Anyone who has lived any length of time at all has paid tuition to life for the lessons it has taught. Because of their experience adults can be resources for learning. Adults are not too excited about learning subject matters that may possibly be applied in several years. They are attracted to problem-centered learning; they want help in dealing with the tasks they must perform as adults.

Adults are not too excited about learning subject matters that may possibly be applied in several years. They are attracted to problem-centered learning; they want help in dealing with the tasks they must perform as adults.

Andragogical norms should govern what happens in the education of adults, particularly in non-degree and voluntary programs of learning. Adult learners and the teacher of adults should work together collaboratively; the teacher of adults should not mount the pedagogical pedestal. Educational planning should involve the adult learners; adults should have some input into determining the content of a course of study and this content should be based on their self-identified needs. Goals of a course of study should be determined mutually by the teacher and by the learners. Learning activities should emphasize sharing rather than transmission of ideas from teacher to learners. Assessment of educational outcomes should also be a mutual endeavor of teacher and learners.

The previous contrast between pedagogical and andragogical approaches distinguishes andragogy from pedagogy in broad terms. Those who wish to explore the concept of andragogy in greater detail should refer to the two books cited earlier. In the remaining pages of this chapter I want to discuss four ideas: 1) the extent to which andragogical approaches have been adopted by adult religious educators, 2) the historical roots of the **pedagogical** treatment of adults, 3) a present contemporary factor contributing to the tendency to treat adults pedagogically, and 4) some arguments against andragogy that I have heard.

ANDRAGOGY TODAY?

To what extent have andragogical approaches been adopted by adult religious educators? The question cannot be answered absolutely and without danger of error. I am able to make a tentative assessment, however, on the basis of my experience, correspondence, and conversations with many adult religious educators. I suggest that pedagogical approaches far outbalance andragogical approaches in the general field of adult religious education.

More often than not, it is suspected, adult programs are begun without an attempt to determine the real needs of prospective participants or the real needs of parishes or local churches. Needs are usually ascribed to prospective program participants by the clergy or by the director of religious education, and one is inclined to believe that this ascribing of needs takes place almost randomly and without any system.

Program planning is done almost entirely by the clergy or directors of religious education. Collaborative planning with the prospective program participants is almost unheard of.

It is suspected also that much of the religious education of adults is transmissive and appropriative. Authority-figure teachers transmit information and adult learners sponge it up. The model for the teacher, in many instances, is the "preacher" model: the authority speaks and the learners listen.

Programs of adult religious education usually have a subject-matter instead of a problem-centered focus. A biblical theme is selected as a basis for program development, for example, not because such a theme may help learners solve immediate problems but because a usable textbook on the theme has appeared or because a filmstrip has been reviewed by the director of religious education. Quite frequently the controlling variable in the development of programs is the availability of

More often than not, it is suspected, adult programs are begun without an attempt to determine the real needs of prospective participants or the real needs of parishes or local churches.

34

It is my opinion, then, that andragogy is not a major force in
adult religious education today.
This is not to say, however, that
I am pessimistic about the
present state of adult religious
education. On the contrary, I am
optimistic.

Teacher-dominated adult education, transmissive and appropriative forms of education,
pedagogical adult education, I
offer, can be traced back even
in primitive times.

material resources. It is a common mistake to build programs around things rather than around the needs of program participants.

It is my opinion, then, that andragogy is not a major force in adult religious education today. This is not to say, however, that I am pessimistic about the present status of adult religious education. On the contrary, I am optimistic.

First of all, at the national level the adult religious education movement—in Protestant, Anglican, Orthodox, and Roman Catholic churches—is blessed with a growing number of leaders who have recognized the necessity of improving programs for adults.

Secondly, at the regional level there are multitudes of concerned adult religious educators who are in decision-making positions. These educators are arranging a significant number of workshops utilizing the expertise of professional adult educators. More and more professional adult educators from the various universities are being called upon as consultants. It would take the fingers of many hands, I think, to count the times Malcolm Knowles has been invited to conduct workshops or act as consultant for religious educators.

Thirdly, many teachers of adults at the level of the parish or local church are willing to learn how to organize and implement andragogical programs for adults. In last analysis, this may be the biggest reason for optimism.

Briefly, the future of andragogy in adult religious education is very promising.

PEDAGOGY AND ADULTS: THE ROOTS

How did it ever happen that adults began to be treated as children? Knowles suggests that pedagogy in adult education came to the fore in the Dark Ages and that pedagogical approaches to adult education were prominent in the monastic schools as a form of social control over novices in the monastic orders.[3]

While admitting the likelihood of this explanation I must view the matter from what I think is a broader perspective.

Teacher-dominated adult education, transmissive and appropriative forms of education, **pedagogical** adult education, I offer, can be traced back even in primitive times. In quasi-absolutist partriarchal cultures and in oral-aural cultures, the

[3]*Ibid.,* p. 42.

lore of the tribe was passed on intact over the campfires. One of the largest concerns of the hearers was to memorize what was told them by the shamans and tribal storytellers. At all costs the great deeds and symbols of the past were to be preserved and transmitted to future generations.

In monarchical societies the serfs were instructed pedagogically for a very good reason: the kings wanted to exert control over them. Kings, by and large, were not interested in treating people as mature and responsible persons. Mature and responsible persons have ideas of their own and are not always content with the status quo. Monarchs were concerned principally with issuing mandates and keeping people in a state of political dependency. It is my contention, therefore, that the entire socio-political structure of societies supported the pedagogical treatment of adults in educational settings. The political model was father of the educational model.

At times certain individuals appeared and began treating adults andragogically. These individuals ran counter to the conventional wisdom and to the norms of absolutist systems. As a consequence they paid the price exacted from those whose status depended on keeping adults as children.

Historically, then, and politically, reasons can be adduced to explain why pedagogy became the accepted manner of relating to adults educationally.

THE HABIT OF PEDAGOGY

In the present time there is another reason why adults are treated as small children in educational settings. Pedagogy is addictive; it is habit-forming.

One observer has pointed out that schools have a dual concern: 1) the school is responsible for the transmission of culture, for the handing out of what is known, for conveying of skills, coding systems, and specific socially defined behaviors, and 2) the school is responsible also for assisting the learner to act individually as an interpreter of culture, as a total person who is able to respond creatively to what is transmitted.[4]

When a child enters first grade it is assumed that he needs contacts with his culture; he needs to know what is already known to prevent him from attempting to recreate the wheel; he needs to know how to communicate and what behaviors are

[4] Eisner, Elliot W., "Instructional and Expressive Objectives," in W. J. Popham (ed.), *Instructional Objectives,* Chicago: Rand-McNally, 1969.

expected of him. The easiest way to get him to learn these things is by transmission techniques: he is told what to do, how to do it, and why it is to be done.

We teach the way we were taught. The very first and impact-filled exposure to teaching that all of us had was exposure to pedagogical approaches. The first image we entertained about "teacher" was "one who tells me something." It is not altogether unreasonable to assume that this image has been carried over into adult years. Many teachers of adults teach pedagogically because they have been exposed initially and most often to this way of teaching.

Pedagogy is addictive for another reason: it is easier to practice pedagogy than andragogy. It is easier to tell somebody something than it is to watch that person struggle to discover; it is easier to take an egotrip at the expense of students than to be a collaborator with them; it is easier to work in a highly structured situation than it is to work in a flexible situation; it is easier to make unilateral decisions than it is to make group decisions. For a thousand and one reasons it is easier to be a pedagogue than it is to be an andragogue.

For a thousand and one reasons it is easier to be a pedagogue than it is to be an andragogue.

ARGUMENTS AGAINST ANDRAGOGY

The final section of this chapter will discuss some arguments that have been raised against the concept of andragogy.

Argument 1: Human nature is essentially the same whether a person is a child or an adult. What is essentially the same should be treated in essentially the same manner. Therefore, both children and adults should be dealt with in essentially the same manner. There is no need for two sets of norms: the pedagogical and the andragogical.

Argument 2: Andragogy proclaims the value of self-directed learning. Self-directed learning is just as necessary for children as for adults. Therefore, andragogy is not specifically applicable to adult education. Why pretend, then, that there is a specific technology for dealing with adults?

Argument 3: The development of the term "andragogy" represents simply the development of another item in the jargon of educationese. There is no reason to multiply terms without reason. The language of educationese is already too ponderous. We need neither andragogy nor a cult of andragogy.

Argument 4: The concept of andragogy developed out of a false application of democratic principles to education. While all people are equal before the law and should have equal opportunities, not all people are intellectually equal. Not all adults are intellectually equipped to determine educational goals, for example. There is **de facto** an intellectual aristocracy. In the realm of education those who are more competent should teach and make decisions; those who are not yet competent should learn and follow the decisions of the teachers.

Response 1: It is true that children and adults share the same human nature and are essentially the same; they are human beings. But it is quite beside the point to argue, therefore, that they should be treated in the same, exact way educationally.

Adults and children are **essentially** the same but **existentially** they are different. The idea of "child" and the idea of "adult" may be joined under the same generic idea of "human being." But there is more to life than the world of ideas.

In the concrete order of reality, in the here-and-now workaday world, the behaviors, responsibilities, experiences, duties, tasks, and functions of adults and children are different. So different, in fact, that a theory for dealing specifically with adult learners is required. This theory is being developed under the name of andragogy. Andragogical principles are being developed for use in the real world and not for ivory-tower isolates who like to play speculative games.

Andragogical principles are being developed for use in the real world and not for ivory-tower isolates who like to play speculative games.

Response 2: Argument 2 is not an argument against andragogy at all, but a statement that stresses the need to make childhood and adolescent learning more self-directive. If children and adolescents are not treated as self-directing persons to some extent, their drive toward maturity will be affected adversely. If you treat another person with respect, he will become more of a self-respecting person; if you give responsibility for learning to children and adolescents, they will become more responsible persons.

While it is not unreasonable, it is suggested, to use a model of adult education for childhood education (in order to help children become adults), it is reprehensible perhaps to use a model of childhood education (pedagogy) as a model for adult education.

The andraogogical model of education is specifically applicable to adult education. But the model may be extended and applied to some degree to childhood learning. While it is not unreasonable, it is suggested, to use a model of adult education for childhood education (in order to help children become adults), it is reprehensible perhaps to use a model of childhood education (pedagogy) as a model for adult education.

Response 3: Argument 3 is without substance. It is an old debater's trick to tarnish an idea by name calling. Admittedly the language of educators is too often fraught with jargon, but andragogy is not a term that fits in the lexicon of jargon. Jargon is "obscure and pretentious language." If I were to call a snapshot an "item of iconographic reproductive processes," I would be guilty of jargonizing. To call a new idea by a new term is simply logical, especially when the new term distinguishes a new set of assumptions and behaviors from the old. To speak of the "pedagogy of adult education" is patently misleading.

The belief that there actually is an intellectually elite is ungrounded. If such a group of intellectually elite people can be located anywhere, I would like to know where they can be found—and on what grounds others than self-proclamation they have been nominated as members of the intellectual aristocracy.

Response 4: The idea that an intellectual elite should control the educational directions of so-called subordinate people is both arrogant and paternalistic. The belief that there actually is an intellectually elite is ungrounded. If such a group of intellectually elite people can be located anywhere, I would like to know where they can be found—and on what grounds other than self-proclamation they have been nominated as members of the intellectual aristocracy.

Approaches to adult education which dictate that one group of people should determine the educational content and goals for another group of people run counter to one of the main purposes of education: education should be a freeing experience; it should be liberating. Education cannot be fully liberating where the adult learners are not permitted a voice in determining goals, goal paths, and contents.

Besides, in a situation where adults volunteer for learning, the elitist approach to education simply does not work. To treat adults as children is an affront to adult autonomy. Not many adults will tolerate such an insult. They will vote with their feet: they simply will not participate in the educational programs that have been arranged for them by their "superiors."

CONCLUSION

Priests, ministers, and directors of religious education particularly must be conscious of the need to behave andragogically in planning and implementing educational programs. They are ordinarily treated with so much deference by people that it is easy for them to fall into the trap of pedagogical behavior and attitudes. Teachers of adults should frequently examine their consciences in terms of the andragogy/pedagogy contrast.

Andragogy is a new idea for new times. New times are upon us and we need new ideas, new theories, new fundamental principles if we are to shape the contours of the future. Continued utilization of pedagogical approaches in adult religious education will spell out educational disaster; use of andragogical approaches will mean the revitalization of adult religious education.

5. Things You Should Know About Adult Learners

In the opening song of *The Music Man* Professor Howard Hill and his fellow salesmen emphasized, "You Gotta Know Your Territory." Salesmen are not effective unless they know something about prospective buyers: their needs, patterns of behavior, characteristics, and qualities Similarly, teachers of adults in religious education programs should know something about the clients who are to benefit from the educational services provided.

A knowledge of some of the characteristics of adults as learners will enable the religious educator to design and implement instructional activities that are effective and realistic. Lacking this knowledge the teacher of adults runs the risk of treating adult learners pedagogically, the risk of relating to adults as children.

In this final chapter of the foundations section I shall offer and explain briefly ten selected characteristics of adults that should be kept in mind by teachers. The characteristics outlined in this chapter do not, of course, apply universally to all adults; these characteristics, however, may be attributed typically to adult learners.

1. Adults can learn.

It is a prevailing fallacy among many adults themselves that "You can't teach an old dog new tricks." As an erstwhile trainer of dogs, I would dispute the truth of the popular adage. But such a concern need not bother us here because adults are not dogs.

In a previous chapter in this section I referred to Paul Bergevin's affirmation of the adult as learner. This affirmation deserves restatement here. Research and studies in adult education have shown that the loss of adult ability to learn is marginal. Adults have substantial learning capacities well into old age. The decline of the ability to learn in some content areas from early to older adulthood is measurable but insignificant. Indeed, in some areas of study older adults perform better than younger people. This may be attributed to the experience and more mature judgment of older adults.

Research and studies in adult education have shown that the loss of adult ability to learn is marginal. Adults have substantial learning capacities well into old age.

42

The "old dogs/new tricks" motto is employed largely as an empty excuse by adults who do not wish to participate in educational activities and is not a valid reason to discontinue lifelong learning. Sometimes the excuse is articulated to gloss over other reasons the adult may have for not wanting to participate in an educational experience. Acting in the role of counselor the adult educator may uncover the real reason for non-attendance by friendly conversation and empathetic listening.

Those who use the motto to excuse themselves from providing educational offerings for adults in the parish or local church setting, I suggest, really feel insecure when dealing with adult learners. They prefer to work with children because children are more easily controlled.

2. Adult learners are experienced.

An adult is a repository of much information and knowledge that has been "picked up" randomly. As a person moves through life he learns, even if he does not present himself in a formal educational setting. Unless a person is unimaginably obtuse, he will gain much information and knowledge by the mere fact of living in association with others.

This implies that members of a group of adult learners may serve as educational resources for one another. Not a few adult programs have proven successful without material resources such as books, films, filmstrips, etc. Once adults have been organized into a collaborative learning group they are likely to gain much information and knowledge through the process of sharing with one another; members of a collaborative learning group educate one another. As an organizer of such a group the teacher of adults functions principally in the role of facilitator: he takes care of administrative chores and provides a structured occasion for learning.

The religious educator of adults would do well to realize that the most important resources for learning available for adult education are the adults who participate in educational activities. While I recognize the importance of material resources in education as instruments for teaching and learning, I must underscore the importance of perceiving adult learners as human resources for one another in a learning group. Too many teachers, I feel, have depended so heavily on gadgetry and mechanical techniques that they have not utilized human resources (especially the learners) fully and properly.

Once adults have been organized into a collaborative learning group they are likely to gain much information and knowledge through the process of sharing with one another; members of a collaborative learning group educate one another.

3. Adult learners are independent.

The fact that children are perceived as inexperienced and dependent on adults does much to shape the teaching-learning process in childhood education as a process that is teacher-dominated. Perhaps such a situation is unavoidable given the psychological dynamics of the relationship between an adult teacher and learners who are children. But perceptions of learners as dependent must not be carried over into adult education.

Recognition of adult independence should provide a direction for adult education that is different from the direction taken in childhood education. Adult learning activities, particularly in a setting where the adults volunteer for learning, should be participant-centered. Or, as I have indicated in a previous chapter, Knowles' concept of andragogy is applicable instead of the traditional concept of pedagogy.

Adults have minds of their own; they have set opinions and beliefs. Simple pronouncements on the part of the teacher will not change these opinions and beliefs. If educational change is to take place, adults themselves must be involved in the change process. The role of the teacher of adults in many situations is principally the role of the facilitator who arranges the conditions of educational change.

If educational change is to take place, adults themselves must be involved in the change process.

4. Adults look for practical consequences.

Most adults feel that knowledge and information of a purely abstract and speculative nature is not as important as knowledge and information that touches them directly and immediately in their lives. I do not agree that theoretical knowledge is less important than practical knowledge, but the fact is that this is the way most adults feel. Adult learners ordinarily expect to be able to apply what they learn almost immediately to real life; they are concerned with the concrete fruits of learning.

In designing courses and in implementing the teaching-learning process the teacher of adults should raise such questions as, "How can the content of this unit be applied to our lives in the workaday world?" and, "What will be the practical consequences of this knowledge once we have left the formal stituation of learning?"

When planning a course and organizing time frames for learning activities, the teacher should allow time for discussions

44

For many adults the strategies of applying learning are more important than what is learned.

of the immediate "payoffs" from the learning that took place. For many adults the strategies of applying learning are more important than what is learned.

5. Adult learners want to be respected.

Most adults who enroll in voluntary educational programs offered by parishes and local churches fulfill many important roles in the home and in the business world. They have grown accustomed to signs of respect bestowed on them by their friends, neighbors, and co-workers. They are accustomed, in many ways, to egalitarian relationships. Friends and co-workers treat them as equals.

The implications of this for teachers of adults are obvious. The teacher of adults who is a martinet, who has pretensions to superiority, or who "lords it over" adult learners can never be effective. The teacher of adults must consider himself a co-learner with participants in adult programs; he must deal with adults on a plane of equality and must possess a deep respect for the experience and relative maturity of adult learners.

What I am saying may be put in other terms: adults live and work in a democratic society; the adult classroom must be a microcosm of that democratic society. The teacher of adults who attempts to be a feudal autocrat will fail miserably.

What I am saying may be put in other terms: adults live and work in a democratic society; the adult classroom must be a microcosm of that democratic society. The teacher of adults who attempts to be a feudal autocrat will fail miserably. As McLuhan has noted, the past went that-away. There was a time, perhaps, and a place in the past where teachers could posture as "masters" while adult learners took the role of deferential pupils. But that time is no more.

6. Adults are relatively mature and responsible.

In childhood education the teacher determines what is to be studied, when it will be studied, and how it will be studied. While this approach is not always valuable even in a childhood education, there is at least an excuse for it. Children are perceived as requiring more direction than adults in the educational enterprise.

In industrial training and other forms of quasi-compulsory education, the teacher is more directive because of institutional constraints and rigid time boundaries. But teacher directiveness in voluntary education is usually out of place.

Since adults are relatively responsible and mature persons, they should be brought into the planning stages of educational activities as much as possible. They should be invited to collaborate with the teacher in setting goals for learning, selecting educational methods and techniques, and determining resources for learning. The judgment of adult learners should also be highly respected when the time comes to evaluate the educational activity.

7. Adults participate for many reasons.

Research has shown that adults enroll in volunteer educational programs for a number of reasons. Some adults are interested in learning itself. Sometimes the content of a course appears attractive to the adult learner. Other adults are interested in achieving some goal in life and need further education to attain this goal. Education is perceived as an end in itself by those who are interested in learning itself and as a means to an end by those who are goal oriented. Still other adults are interested simply in the activity that surrounds participation in an educational program: social interaction with new friends and acquaintances, for example. A number of adults, of course, probably have mixed motivations; they are interested to some extent in learning itself, in goals they can reach by means of education, and in initiating social contacts with others.

To meet these general orientations of adult learners the educational offering not only should deal with the manifest content of the course, but should also enable learners to apply the content to their lives and should provide a climate which encourages people to develop friendly relations with one another.

This last matter—the matter of social climate—is important and often neglected. At the first meeting of adult learners a sufficient amount of time should be blocked off so that participants will be able to introduce themselves and discover the background of their co-learners. Social interchange may also be supported by keeping the instructional situation informal and relaxed.

This last matter—the matter of social climate—is important and often neglected.

8. Adult learners expect physical comfort.

Trifles are never trifling in adult education. There should be an easy access to the place of instruction; adults should not be expected to climb four flights of stairs to get to their classrooms. The temperature of the room should be carefully moderated. Lighting should be adequate because of the decline of adult visual acuity. Adults should not be asked to sit in chairs or desks that have been designed for children.

When children are uncomfortable with the physical context for learning they usually create disciplinary problems or suffer in silence. Adults are different. They simply refuse to return to a situation where they have been physically discomforted. The easy chair in front of the home TV, like a siren call, beckons adults who have been seated in undersized desks, and in a cold and poorly lighted classroom.

The teacher of adults should check occasionally into the matter of the physical comfort of the learners. If he finds that the place of instruction is perceived as too noisy, too warm or cold, too difficult to get to, too small, etc., he should remedy the causes of discomfort.

9. Adults may not always attend.

Adults have many obligations associated with family life, social life, and work. These obligations sometimes take a higher priority than attendance at educational activities. If a mother has a choice between attending to a sick child or attending a Tuesday night class, she will logically, and rightly, stay with her child.

Anticipating obstacles to consistent adult attendance, the teacher will attempt to organize class sessions so that each session is integral and whole in itself.

Anticipating obstacles to consistent adult attendance, the teacher will attempt to organize class sessions so that each session is integral and whole in itself. When it is necessary to establish continuity between one class session and another, the teacher should present a review of what has taken place previously. A review of past learning activities is helpful in any case because such a review serves to reorient the learners and gives them a sense of direction.

10. Adults sometimes resist change.

Many adults are fairly well set in their ways. It takes effort to change behavior or attitudes and adults do not always want to expend this effort. Adults sometimes romanticize the past as "the good old days" and need time to adjust to new ways of doing things, to new ideas, and to new insights.

The teacher of adults should not be discouraged when he cannot measure the immediate effects of an educational activity. He should make haste slowly when attempting to facilitate change in areas of life that are laden with emotions and deep feelings. Adults can learn and they can change. But the teacher of adults must be patient.

The teacher of adults should not be discouraged when he cannot measure the immediate effects of an educational activity. He should make haste slowly when attempting to facilitate change in areas of life that are laden with emotions and deep feelings. Adults can learn and they can change. But the teacher of adults must be patient.

CONCLUSION

In English composition courses and in public speaking courses, it is usually advised that the learners develop a "sense of audience." Having taught both composition and public speaking, I could always separate the performance of learners into two categories (excellent and marginal) on the basis of the learners' sense of audience. Good writers always ask the question, "How will the readers interpret and react to what I have written?" Effective speakers ask the question, "Will my spoken words be understood by those who hear me?" Marginal performance can almost always be attributed to a lack of a sense of audience on the part of the writer or speaker. Speakers and writers who have not studied the recipients of their messages do not communicate effectively.

A sense of audience, I think, is what generally separates an excellent teacher from a marginal teacher. The teacher who has developed a sense of audience tends to be self-critical and reflective as regards the educational procedures he employs. He is always "putting himself in the shoes" of the learners; he attempts to perceive his classroom behavior the way the learners perceive this behavior.

A sense of audience, I think, is what generally separates an excellent teacher from a marginal teacher.

To be sure, not all groups of adult learners are alike. But adults do share certain general characteristics regardless of the group in which they find themselves. Attention to these characteristics represents the beginning of the development of a sense of the adult audience. In this chapter I have tried to outline some of the more important characteristics of adult learners. Readers may wish to refer to Kidd's *How Adults Learn*[1] and Bischof's *Adult Psychology,*[2] for a more detailed analysis of the adult as learner.

Many religious educators who have previously and successfully functioned as teachers of children are preparing themselves for educational work with adults. This preparation is greatly needed. Because of previous classroom experiences in childhood education some religious educators may lack an appropriate sense of the adult audience. The development of this sense is crucial, I suggest, if these religious educators are to make a smooth transition from childhood to adult education.

[1] Kidd, J.R., *How Adults Learn,* New York: Association Press, 1973.

[2] Bischof, Ledford, *Adult Psychology,* New York: Harper and Row, 1969.

6. Building a Total Program: A Blueprint

Many educational programs for adults are developed on the spur of the moment, haphazardly, and with little regard for systematic planning. Some kind of systematic planning is required, however, if educational programs are to be fruitful in terms of adult learning. It is better to plan than not to plan for the simple reason that human endeavors are more properly managed when they are based on critical, farsighted rationality rather than on impulsive decisions.

In this chapter I shall outline a model for the development of a total program in the parish or local church setting. By "total program" I mean a complex of courses, a curriculum, or a series of educational activities that spans a time frame of several weeks. Such activities are usually known as "the Fall program," "the Lenten program," and so forth.

A program development model is a conceptual framework for sorting out and organizing the tasks involved in developing an educational program. A model is a blueprint or a design. It is an outline of a step-by-step procedure. Models are ordinarily generic; that is, they identify the **major** steps that must be taken in the developmental process.

Program developers should not follow any program development slavishly. Those who use program development models should not hesitate to manipulate the steps in the model to suit the purposes of specific situations. In other words, the program development model presented in this chapter may be modified to meet the requirements of a particular context.

THE MODEL

Each of the parts of the program development model will be listed; a brief discussion of each of the stages will then follow. follow.

Program Development Model

1. Organize an adult education council.
2. Recruit leaders and teachers.
3. Formulate a brief statement of philosophy and policy.
4. Determine the educational needs of prospective learners.

5. List the anticipated outcomes of the program.
6. Determine the content of the program.
7. Organize subject matter through content grouping.
8. Select appropriate methods and techniques.
9. Itemize the human and material resources that are required.
10. Define the space-time context of the program.
11. Arrange for the promotion of the program.
12. Design a procedure for evaluation.

THE ADULT EDUCATION COUNCIL

Every parish or local church should have a permanent adult education council. The full-time business of this council should relate to the adult education programming that takes place during the year. Members of the adult education council need not have any special expertise. They must be committed, however, to adult education and manifest a willingness to work for program development and improvement.

The chief work of the adult education council is to assist the program developer in carrying out the tasks of program development, to help the program developer formulate a working philosophy for the program, and to aid the program developer in preparing policies for the program.

LEADERS/TEACHERS

Those who will probably serve as leaders and teachers of the various courses in the program should be brought into the program development process at an early stage. There is a problem here, however. Suppose seven leaders are recruited by the program developer and are asked to take responsibility for course offerings. Suppose further that the needs assessment (which will be explained later) reveals that there is no need for the services of three of the leaders. These leaders are not interested in the topics that will meet the needs of the prospective learners. Indeed, it may happen that some of the recruited leaders have little competency in the subject-matter areas that are identified through the needs assessment as likely subject-matter areas for a program. Should such a dilemma occur it may be resolved by appointing the leaders to the adult education council. The program developer, leaders/teachers, and members of the adult education council will work together, in any event, in the program development process.

Leaders and teachers are recruited early in the program development process because they should be involved in the process as fully as possible. Those who anticipate teaching a course or leading a group discussion on a particular topic may have valuable information to contribute to the program development process.

PHILOSOPHY AND POLICY

The word "philosophy" is amenable to different definitions. As the word is used here it means a set of beliefs about education, how adults should be treated in the educational situation, what is the ideal relationship between teacher and learners in adult education, how active participation of the learners in the instructional process can be facilitated, and so forth.

Educational programs for adults are sometimes established without a philosophical undergirding, and this is like building castles on shifting sands. Educational programs must have a philosophical foundation. If questions pertaining to educational philosophy are not asked (or answered) prior to the development of a program, there will result a general confusion concerning the overarching purposes of the program.

Policies are general norms that are accepted as standards of operation for the program. A policy attempts to delineate guidelines that may be useful in the administration of the program. Policies sometimes try to anticipate problems and difficulties before they happen, and outline ways these problems and difficulties may be handled.

It is not necessary to compile a huge handbook of educational philosophy and an encyclopedic collection of policies. Philosophical principles may be stated in a brief fashion outlining the nature of adult education, the general goals of adult religious education, the ideal resources and means to be used to accomplish these goals, and general principles that guide instructors in the instructional situation. One of the statements of philosophy for a program, for example, may concern the offering of so-called secular courses in the adult religious education program, e.g., focusing on courses that are religious by reason of intent and not content.

Likewise, a list of general program policies need not be lengthy. It should be determined, for example, whether people will be permitted to enroll in a course offering if they have missed the first several sessions, whether instructors will be remunerated for their services, whether a tuition fee will be charged, etc. Policies are more specific than philosophical principles and usually relate to program administration. Quite frequently policies involve budgetary considerations.

NEEDS

There are two types of needs that must be considered in every educational program: institutional and individual needs.

The educational program, if it is sponsored by a church, should meet some institutional needs. Persons are members of communities; they should be prepared to meet some of the community needs of which they may be unaware. Community officials (in this case pastors and ministers) should be asked to ascribe needs to the prospective participants in the program. These needs should be listed; the program should in some way attempt to meet these needs.

Adults will not involve themselves in an educational program with a sense of commitment unless the issues addressed by the program speak to their individual needs also. In terms of individual needs, the educational program should deal with subject areas that are need-satisfying for the learners.

There are many ways to determine the individual educational needs of prospective learners. The program developer may wish to interview a randomly selected sample of prospective learners; he may decide to construct a brief questionnaire which will enable prospective learners to list the topics that appeal to them. In every case, however, some attempt must be made to identify individual educational needs. The program that is concerned only with institutional needs has little hope of success.

A subsequent chapter in this volume will discuss the needs assessment procedure in greater detail.

ANTICIPATED OUTCOMES

Once a list of needs has been compiled, the program developer should select the educational needs that are to be addressed by the program and list the anticipated outcomes of the program.

One of the most effective ways to give direction to a program, and to preserve it from vagueness and aimlessness, is to list anticipated outcomes of the program before the program is implemented. Anticipated outcomes of the program may be formulated in general terms; anticipated outcomes or objectives for the courses comprising the program should be stated with some degree of specificity.

Anticipated program outcomes should be formuated with reference to post-program understandings, attitudes, and skills that will be possessed by the participants. Anticipated outcomes should deal with the terminal competencies of the learners and

Adults will not involve themselves in an educational program with a sense of commitment unless the issues addressed by the program speak to their individual needs also. In terms of individual needs, the educational program should deal with subject areas that are need-satisfying for the learners.

not with woolly expressions of what the instructors are going to do during the program.

The formulation of anticipated outcomes will help the instructors and program developer focus more exactly on the aims of the program, and will program a basis for the later evaluation of the program.

Content or Subject Areas

By "content" is meant the issues and ideas that will be treated in the program. The content of an educational program is derived, of course, from the needs to be satisfied by the program and from the anticipated outcomes.

It happens as a matter of course that most programs are developed around one or two material resources such as books or magazines. Textbooks and filmstrips are chosen, for example, and then the program is planned.

Educational programs should not be initiated for the purpose of teaching the content of some worthwhile textbooks. Educational programs should be initiated for the purpose of providing content that satisfies the needs of **this** group of learners. To select a textbook and then proceed to build a program is to place the cart before the horse, and it is no wonder such carts do not move forward.

Educational programs should be initiated for the purpose of providing content that satisfies the needs of *this* group of learners. To select a textbook and then proceed to build a program is to place the cart before the horse, and it is no wonder such carts do not move forward.

Content Grouping

After a list has been made of the main ideas that will be treated in the program, the ideas should be grouped in "families." Each family then becomes a course offering, a workshop, a general topic for group discussions, and so forth. A needs assessment may turn up fifteen different educational needs; there may be fifteen anticipated outcomes for the program. But a number of these needs may be addressed by one course offering. Five of the fifteen needs may be met by offering one course of six sessions; another five of the needs may be met by conducting a weekend workshop. One of the needs may be met at a single meeting; three of the needs may be met by forming a discussion group that will meet for ten Tuesday evenings; the final need may be met by independent reading.

The process of content grouping does not concern the selection of formats for learning but merely putting ideas together into clusters. The example provided above of the fifteen needs is intended to illustrate how several similar educational needs may be grouped together under one heading.

Appropriate Methods and Techniques

After the subject matter or content of the program has been organized in different "families," appropriate methods and techniques must be selected. The difference between a method and a technique should be noted. According to Verner[1] a method is institutionally centered; it is an administrative function. A technique is participant centered and is a function of the learning situation. Under individual methods Verner lists: a) correspondence study, b) directed individual study, c) apprenticeship, and d) internship. Correspondence study needs no further explication. Individual study is study on a tutorial basis, e.g., an instructor outlines reading materials for the learner and discusses the books with the learner. In the apprenticeship method the learner participates in an educational situation under the supervision of the instructor for the purpose of acquiring skills and knowledge. In the internship method the learner participates in an educational situation under the supervision of the instructor for the purpose of integrating and applying previously learned skills and knowledge.

Verner further suggests that group methods are of two kinds: methods for small groups and methods for large groups. Small group methods would be: a) the class, b) the discussion group, c) the laboratory (experiential learning); large group methods would be: a) the assembly (workshop) and b) the convention. Once the methods have been determined for handling "families" of subject matter, attention should be directed to the selection of possible techniques to use within the framework of the chosen methods.

A later chapter will describe various techniques that may be used. It will be sufficient to note here some examples of techniques to clear the distinction between method and technique. Techniques are of two kinds: a) instrumental and b) non-instrumental. Instrumental techniques employ the use of mechanical devices or printed materials: filmstrips, overhead projections, games, pencil and paper exercises, etc. Non-instrumental techniques principally arrange those in the teaching-learning situation in different patterns for communication: role plays, panels, forums, lectures, symposia, and so forth.

While it is absolutely necessary in developing a total program to identify the methods to be used, it is not necessary to list

[1] Verner, Coolie, *A Conceptual Scheme for the Identification and Classification of Processes,* Adult Education Association of the USA, 1962, p. 9.

techniques. Techniques are utilized within the framework of a method and are usually selected by individual teachers/leaders. The adult education council, however, may wish to suggest some possible techniques that could be used within the structures of the methods that are determined. It may be suggested, for example, that a particular "family" of subject matters or general topic be treated in a class situation. The adult education council may also wish to indicate the advisability of using the field trip as a technique to be used in this class (method).

Human and Material Resources

There are two orders of resources that may possibly come into play in educational programs: human resources and material resources. Human resources may be guest speakers, for example, who are employed in the educational program. Under the rubric of material resources may be classed textbooks, filmstrips, overhead transparencies, etc.

Human and material resources are marshalled together only after needs have been identified and content has been selected and organized. Most programs **begin** with the marshalling of human and material resources and as a consequence are not need-satisfying.

A written list of required human and material resources should be compiled at this stage of program development.

Most programs *begin* with the marshalling of human and material resources and as a consequence are not need-satisfying.

Space-Time Context

Space-times contextual planning takes place when the program developer arranges a place for the learners to meet, and schedules educational episodes in time modules. This kind of planning responds to the following questions: a) When shall this group meet? b) How often shall the group meet? c) Where shall the group meet? d) What will be the duration of the sessions?

At this stage of program development, for example, the program may include two eight-week series, a weekend workshop, a field-trip, and four discussion groups. Space-time planning for such a program will be quite a task.

Program Promotion

Once the contours of the total program have been delineated on paper, it is then necessary to plan for the promotion of the program. Personal contact, telephone contact, announcements in church, announcements in the church bulletin, distribution of special handouts, mailouts; all of these approaches may be used to promote and publicize the program. Promotional planning should be completed well in advance of the implementation of the program.

Much promotion is done, incidentally, at an earlier stage of program development: the stage of needs assessment. If individual needs are determined adequately, many adults will seek to satisfy these needs by means of participation in the educational program.

Evaluation

Program improvement can come about only through evaluation. Lacking evaluation, educational programs have a tendency to stagnate. In one sense, then, evaluation is the most important part of program development.

Program improvement can come about only through evaluation. Lacking evaluation, educational programs have a tendency to stagnate. In one sense, then, evaluation is the most important part of program development.

In educational programs where learners volunteer as participants the results of tests are not ordinarily used to determine if educational objectives or anticipated outcomes have been realized. Usually the evaluation of volunteer programs is carried out in terms of learner satisfaction. If the participants in an educational program look upon their experiences in the program with a measure of satisfaction, the program is probably meeting its goals. More will be written about evaluation in another chapter in this volume.

Conclusion

Program development is a complex process. What has been presented above by way of a blueprint of the process is a mere outline of the tasks involved in program development. Some of the more complicated tasks in the outline will be discussed in more detail in subsequent chapters.

Because program development is so complicated and arduous, it is advised that the program developer and adult education council engage in planning activities well before the program is initiated. Planning for a Fall program, for example, should begin in the preceding Spring; planning for a Lenten program should begin in the preceding Fall.

The planning procedure recommended here is time consuming and involves a great deal of work. It is much easier to "throw" a program together with little planning; it is much easier to allow educational programs for adults to grow up "like Topsy." Anything worth doing, as we are reminded by the old saw, is worth doing right. It is not my suggestion that the planning procedure offered here is **the** right way of program development. It is, however, **a** right way among many right ways; a "way" that promises improved adult education programs.

7. Assessing Needs and Interests: Q's & A's

In this chapter attention will be turned to the bedrock of any educational program for adults: adult needs and interests. I shall respond to a series of questions about the assessment of educational needs and interests as a preprogram development strategy. Here are the questions:

1. Why should a need/interest assessment be conducted prior to the development of a program?

2. What is an educational need? An interest?

3. What is an ascribed educational need? An ascertained educational need?

4. When should the need/interest assessment be conducted?

5. Whose needs/interests should be assessed?

6. Who are the sources of data regarding educational needs/interests?

7. What are some techniques for collecting data regarding educational needs/interests?

8. How long should the survey instruments be that are used to collect need/interest data?

9. How can survey instruments be delivered to people and how can completed survey instruments be returned?

10. Is it necessary to conduct a need/interest assessment before the development of every program?

Why?

Most adults will not volunteer for learning if the educational program is perceived by them as irrelevant and meaningless **for**

58

them. An educational program may concern some highly important issues but if these issues do not strike a responsive chord in potential adult learners, the program will not be well attended.

The key word is "motivation." People will be moved to enroll and participate in an educational program when the content of the program satisfies some needs or concerns some interests of the people. The question, then, is not about the relevance of the program but concerns the **perceived relevance** of the program. If an educational program—or individual course offerings within the total program—is perceived as need-satisfying or interesting, incentives for participation in the program will be present.

Need/interest assessments are conducted prior to the development of an educational program to discover the educational needs and interests of potential program participants, It is very simple to pull topics for an educational program "out of a hat," but this kind of magic does not work in the long haul.

What?

An educational need is some lack or deficiency that hinders a person from reaching a goal; the lack or deficiency can be filled by educational means.

If I wish to travel from point A to point B, I must have the ability to do so. Lacking this ability or knowledge of a route, I probably shall not reach my goal. If I am unable to travel physically, I may have a physical need; if I am fearful of motion, I may have an emotional or psychological need. If I lack the knowledge of a route, I have an educational need. Needs that can be filled by gaining knowledge, attitudes, or skills are usually called educational needs. Educational needs always have some relation to goals. This is to say, if a person requires a particular understanding, a specific attitude, or a certain skill in order to reach a goal (and if this understanding, attitude, or skill can be gained through education), the person has an educational need.

An educational interest is an orientation toward a specific topic or issue, not because the topic or issue will fill some lack, but because a person has a preference for the topic or issue and finds satisfaction in dealing with the topic or issue. Educational interests concern, largely, matters of personal preference or taste. One person may have a taste for studying the religious implications of social problems; another person may prefer to discuss church history; still another person may wish to concern himself with scriptural topics.

How account for interests? An old Latin saying indicates that "in matters of taste there is no room for dispute." Most people cannot explain why they are interested in a particular subject or why they began a particular hobby. They are simply interested in some things and not interested in other things.

It is the task of the program developer to assess both the needs of prospective learners and their interests.

Ascribed and Ascertained Needs/Interests?

If a program developer, in his effort to assess needs/interests, goes to a pastor and asks the pastor to list the needs/interests of the people, the program developer would be gathering data on ascribed needs/interests. If the program developer analyzed books, articles, and other documentation that identified the needs and interests of adults, he would also be gathering data on ascribed needs/interests. An ascribed need or interest is a need or interest attributed to a person by someone else.

It is perfectly legitimate to ascribe needs/interests to potential learners on the basis of interviews with church officials and on the basis of an analysis of books, articles, and other written materials usually known as documentation. Sometimes a pastor will be able to identify an educational need of the people relating to the membership in the parish or local church. The people generally may be unaware of this need because they are more conscious of their needs as individuals than they are of their needs as members of a community.

Care must be taken, however, not to establish a program solely on ascribed needs/interests. It is a difficult thing to pinpoint the needs and interests of other people, even from an "official" vantage point. If individual needs/interests are not assessed prior to the development of a program, the program will not ordinarily attract many participants.

An ascertained need or interest is a need or interest identified by the person who perceives a lack in himself or consciously attributes a particular preference to himself. If a program developer goes to the people and asks them to identify their educational needs/interests, he will be gathering data about ascertained needs. Indeed, he will ascertain particular needs and interests through the need/interest assessment.

In most churches the program developer would do well to spend a great deal of energy in ascertaining the educational needs and interests of potential clients of educational services. I have perceived a tendency in the field of adult religious education to base programs mostly on ascribed needs/interests. This may explain why programs in some places are poorly attended.

It is a difficult thing to pinpoint the needs and interests of other people, even from an "official" vantage point. If individual needs and interests are not assessed prior to the development of a program, the program will not ordinarily attract many participants.

When?

A need/interest assessment should take place several months before the educational program is implemented. It takes a long time to collate the data gathered in an assessment and organize a program. A review of the previous chapter will suggest how complex the process of program development actually is.

Whose Needs/Interests?

Decisions must be made by the program developer and adult education council regarding the "universe" of potential program participants. Are only the members of a local church or parish to be considered potential program participants? Or will the target audience for the educational program be the neighborhood or community at large? If the educational program is being organized for an entire neighborhood population, regardless of religious affiliation, the need/interest assessment will obviously be more time consuming and complex.

If the potential program participants are limited to those who are active members of a church, the need/interest assessment will be less taxing but will still constitute a complex operation. In this regard I must mention a concern. It seems to me that some educational programs sponsored by local churches and parishes are aimed at "saving the saved." The needs and interests of the most active church members—the pillars—are taken into consideration but not much thought is given to those who are marginal church members.

Who Are Data Sources?

A need/interest assessment gathers data about educational needs and interests from different sources: church officials, documentation, and the prospective learners themselves.

It is not too difficult to interview church officials or to analyse documentation in gathering need/interest data. It is problematic, however, assessing the needs/interests of large numbers of people. Suppose, for example, a local church or parish decides to sponsor an educational program that is religious by intent (the content of the program is not religious **per se**) and that the entire population of the community is considered as constituting the potential program participants. Suppose further that the community has a population of 50,000. Will it be necessary to send out 50,000 questionnaires to ascertain the educational needs/interests of the community?

For large scale operations it may be advisable to resort to random sampling to ascertain the needs/interests of adult learners. Random sampling means that everyone in the "universe"—all 50,000 people in the community—has an opportunity of being selected to provide information about his or her needs and interests.

A surprisingly small number of people need to be surveyed in order to gain worthwhile information about needs and interests. If the size of the population is 50,000, only 217 people need respond to a questionnaire. This return would guarantee 98% precision, 99 times out of 100.[1] This is not the place to discuss sampling procedures and statistics. Those who are in positions of responsibility for large scale operations in adult religious education, however, would do well to turn their attention to statistical procedures for ascertaining educational needs and interests. A little more respect for statistical procedures would rescue diocesan, district, or regional programs from perceived irrelevancy.

There is a major drawback in using sampling techniques to ascertain educational needs and interests. When people are surveyed about their educational needs and interests, program promotion has already begun. One of the side effects of a need/interest assessment is the stimulation of interest in the forthcoming program. This side effect does not obtain when sampling techniques are employed.

What Techniques?

Several techniques for data collection regarding needs and interests may be recommended: 1) interview, 2) check list, 3) group discussion, 4) open-ended questionnaire, 5) combination techniques.

Prospective program participants may be interviewed individually to determine their educational needs and interests. They are simply asked to discuss what they would like to see in the proposed program while the interviewer takes notes. The technique is appropriate for gathering data from church officials, but is usually too time-consuming to be used for all of the prospective program participants.

A checklist merely lists twenty or thirty topics or issues. The respondent is asked to place a check mark next to the topics or issues that will meet his needs or interests. The checklist technique is easy to employ for large numbers of people. But the checklist technique also has its drawbacks. It could happen that none of the thirty topics appearing on the checklist meets the needs or interests of the person who is responding to the survey. Who selects the original topics that are to appear on the checklist? Should not the survey respondent be given the

A surprisingly small number of people need to be surveyed in order to gain worthwhile information about needs and interests. If the size of the population is 50,000, only 217 people need respond to a questionnaire.

[1] Slonim, Morris James, *Sampling,* New York: Simon and Schuster, 1960.

opportunity of identifying topics not appearing on the checklist?

Group discussion can generate much data about educational needs and interests. Several groups of people can sit down and "hash out" what they would like to see in the forthcoming educational program. The group discussion technique is particularly useful for gathering data from organizations within the parish or local church. The group discussion technique, however, is not without disadvantage. How can those who do not belong to any organization within the parish or local church be persuaded to sit down for a group discussion on the forthcoming educational program?

An open-ended questionnaire merely asks the respondent to identify what topics should be treated in the forthcoming educational program. It is assumed that in the process of identifying such topics the respondent will also identify his or her needs or interests. The disadvantage: at times people need a list of possible topics to get them started thinking about an educational program. A simple question asking for possible topics does not give any cue or hint to stimulate the thought processes of the respondent.

The best approach, perhaps, to need/interest assessment is the utilization of a combination of data-gathering techniques.

The best approach, perhaps, to need/interest assessment is the utilization of a combination of data-gathering techniques. For example: a number of individuals may be interviewed about what they would like to see in the forthcoming program; several groups may meet for a group discussion to identify possible topics. Using the topics generated through selected interviews and group discussions, a checklist may be compiled. The checklist is distributed to all of the potential program participants. An open-ended question—"In addition to the topics appearing on the checklist, what topics do you think should be covered in the program?"—may be added to the checklist.

How Long?

How long should survey instruments (checklists, questionnaires, etc.) be? Answer: As short as possible.

How long should survey instruments (checklists, questionnaires, etc.) be? Answer: As short as possible. Most adults do not like to take the time to respond to surveys. Several years ago a question was making the rounds: How long should a girl's skirt be? The answer to the question was succinct: Long enough to cover the subject and short enough to be interesting. A need/interest survey should be long enough to gather pertinent data and short enough to avoid being deposited in the nearest wastebasket.

Delivery and Return?

What is the best way to deliver surveys to prospective learners and to assure the return of the completed surveys?

Several approaches may be recommended.

A survey may be mailed to all of the potential program participants. If surveys are to be mailed, a self-addressed, stamped return envelope should be enclosed. While this delivery/return system is excellent for gathering data from large numbers of persons, it is costly in terms of work and postage.

A survey may be distributed in church on Sundays. A box for the return of the surveys may be situated prominently in the church vestibule. Unfortunately, this technique does not reach many people who do not attend church regularly.

Surveys may be distributed at the meetings of church organizations. A member of the organization could be appointed to collect completed surveys. Again, this approach yields data only from those who are actively involved in church affairs.

Simply stated, there is no best way to distribute and collect surveys. If the budget permits, the mail technique is to be advised. It is likely that more data will be gathered using this approach.

How Often?

Must a need/interest assessment be conducted prior to the development of every program? If the need/interest assessment is complete and executed properly, the data generated from the assessment may be used as a basis for the development of several programs. Not all of the needs and interests identified in an assessment can be dealt with in the context of one program.

Need/interest data, however, has a way of growing stale. This is due simply to the fact that adult needs and interests change over given time spans. Assessments should be made every 12 to 18 months.

Conclusion

The assessment of needs and interests is hard work. It is necessary work. I venture to hypothesize that if more adult programs sponsored by parishes and local churches began with an assessment of needs and interests, these programs would prove to be more satisfying to participants and would enroll greater numbers of adults. The only way to test my hypothesis, it seems, is to give need/interest assessment a try.

Since the essays in this volume are introductory in nature, it would be beyond the purpose of the book to detail the procedures involved in need/interest assessment. I can recommend a book, however, for those who wish to pursue the topic further. The book is *The Modern Practice of Adult Education*[2] by Malcolm Knowles.

[2]Knowles, Malcolm, *The Modern Practice of Adult Education,* New York: Association Press, 1971.

8. Planning Instructional Episodes: A Seven-Step Procedure

Within the context of a total adult education program there may be several different course offerings. Remember, the concept of total program as it is used here refers to a series of course offerings or a curriculum. Within the context of a course offering there may be a series of several class sessions. These individual class sessions are called instructional episodes. An instructional episode ordinarily lasts anywhere from 45 minutes to two hours.

In this chapter a seven-step procedure for planning instructional episodes will be presented. The procedure may be used by teachers of adults or by adult discussion groups to structure and organize educational activities. The basic ideas contained in this chapter appear in another form in *Design for Adult Education in the Church*[1] by Paul Bergevin and John McKinley. Bergevin and McKinley offer a six-step planning procedure for program development. A previous chapter in this volume has dealt with the development of the total program and a twelve-step procedure was described. I have taken the Bergevin-McKinley model for program planning, modified the model a bit, added a seventh step, and prepared a model or framework that may be used by teachers for planning instructional units or episodes.

The Need for Planning

Just as there is a need for the systematic planning of the total adult education program, there is a need for the systematic planning of individual educational episodes. Systematic planning assures the best use of available time, gives a direction to class activities, and organizes the teaching-learning process. Some teachers may be able to enter a classroom without a "game plan" and conduct a worthwhile class session. These teachers, however, are in the minority. Most teachers require some kind of outline of what is intended to take place in order to keep the class session from bogging down and eventually becoming a waste of time.

[1] Bergevin, Paul, and McKinley, John, *Design for Adult Education in the Church,* New York: Seabury Press, 1965.

Seven Steps

Here are the seven steps recommended to teachers for planning individual class sessions or instructional episodes:

1. Identify the need/interest to be addressed.

2. Formulate a topical question.

3. Identify the educational objective.

4. Select resources.

5. Select techniques.

6. Formulate an activity outline.

7. State evaluation procedure.

Needs/Interests

A constellation of needs/interests will have been identified by the need/interest assessment conducted prior to program development. Not all of these needs and interests will be able to be treated in the space of one class session. The teacher must identify a particular need or interest of the learners that is to be addressed during the instructional episode. This need or interest should be written out.

If by some chance a needs assessment has not been conducted prior to program development, the teacher must assess the needs and interests of the learners. Once learners have identified a particular need or interest, the teacher writes out the need or interest in the instructional plan.

Topical Question

After an educational need or interest has been identified, the teacher must formulate an instructional topic. The instructional topic should be written in the form of a question. Furthermore, the question should not be answerable by a simple "yes" or "no." Questions that are answerable by a "yes" or "no" are more conducive to debate than to inquiry and dialogue.

The topical question is derived from the stated need or interest. By responding to the topical question the stated need will ideally be met or the stated interest will be adequately covered. Just as the topical question is derived from the stated need/interest, the educational objective of the episode is derived from the topical question.

Educational Objectives

Instructional activities that have no stated objective are liable to become diffuse and unfocused. The educational objective for the instructional episode must be stated clearly and properly.

Different people state educational objectives in different ways. Even professional, full-time teachers find it difficult to state educational objectives properly. For this reason I shall devote several paragraphs to an explanation of how to prepare instructional objectives.

The term "objective" is open to many different interpretations. Suppose we have a group of five teachers. We ask them to respond to the question, "What is the educational objective of your next class session?" Each of the five teachers may respond to the question from a different frame of reference. We might obtain the following answers to our question:

Albert: "My objective is to present an informal talk about the social responsibilities of Christians today."

Betty: "My objective is to deal with the social responsibilities of Christians today."

Carl: "The objective of the class meeting is to offer the learners the opportunity of discussing the social responsibilities of Christians today."

Darlene: "At the conclusion of the class session the learners will understand more about the social responsibilities of Christians today."

Edward: "At the conclusion of the class session the learners will list four social responsibilities of Christians today in a period of seven minutes."

At first glance the statements of the teachers may appear similar. But since each of the teachers interpreted the meaning of "objective" in a different way, each of them stated a truly different kind of objective for the instructional episode. A close scrutiny of the five statements will bear this out.

Albert stated his objective in terms of **teacher activity.** He expressed what he was going to do: present an informal talk. He did not consider what the learners would do during the session or what competencies they would gain as a result of the episode. Albert is in the company of a very large number of teachers. When teachers are asked to formulate objectives they usually think of what **they** are going to do and formulate the objectives around teaching tasks.

When teachers are asked to formulate objectives they usually think of what *they* are going to do and formulate the objectives around teaching tasks.

Betty stated her objective in terms of **topic.** She was concerned mainly with the content of the class session or the subject matter to be treated. She is probably highly content-oriented and does not think too much of what the learners are going to do during the session or about what gains the learners will make. Betty is also representative of a large number of teachers. She is so engrossed—obsessed even—with educational content that she is only slightly aware of teaching procedures, learner tasks, or the competencies to be achieved by the learners.

Carl stated his objective in terms of **learner task.** He pictured mentally what the learners would do **during** the instructional episode. He did not focus on what the learners would know or be able to do as a result of the tasks they completed. Instead of stating an authentic objective Carl simply described the educational activity or learner response that would take place as a reaction to his teaching.

Darlene stated her objective in terms of **general terminal outcome.** She formulated the objective with the learners in mind and expressed the objective in such a way as to describe what would happen to the learners as a result of the instructional episode. When Darlene stated her objective she was concerned with the competencies to be gained by the learners after their experiences within the context of the instructional unit.

Edward is a stickler for measurable outcomes. He stated his objective in terms of **specific terminal outcomes.** He indicated what the learners would be able to do, specifically, as a result of the educational activity. He also included the parameters within which the learners would perform, e.g., "they will list four social responsibilities of Christians today in a period of seven minutes."

The statements of Albert, Betty, and Carl may describe something that will happen during the instructional episode, but essentially these statements do not fill the bill as educational objectives. At any rate, the statements of the trio do not represent what professional educators would call educational objectives.

Edward's objective is proper, but a bit too specific for volunteer learners in a religious education setting. He has stated his objective in **behavioral** terms; this may make some professional educators leap for joy, but it is not necessary given the context of the instructional episode.

Darlene's objective is stated properly, adequately, and realistically. If she wants to test whether the objective has been met, she could formulate a criterion reference (a test item) for the objective, and administer a test at the conclusion of the instructional episode.

Educational objectives, then, must be formulated in terms of the competencies the learners will acquire as a result of the educational activity.

Educational objectives, then, must be formulated in terms of the competencies the learners will acquire as a result of the educational activity.

Resources

The teacher should next list the human and material resources that will be employed in the instructional episode. A guest speaker is a human resource, for example; a filmstrip would be a material resource. Human and material resources that could possibly be utilized should be listed in writing.

Techniques

An educational technique establishes a relationship or linkage between the learners and the subject matter. Various techniques that could possibly be utilized in the instructional episode should be tentatively listed.

Outline

The activity outline budgets the time of the instructional episode. The educational activities that will take place are listed; approximate time frames for each of the activities are identified. In a sense the teacher draws the instructional plan together when he formulates the activity outline.

Evaluation

Adult instructional activities soon become stagnant in the absence of critical assessment. Instructional episodes should be evaluated by the participants continuously during the series of episodes. For example, a teacher is conducting a course which meets for ten consecutive Tuesday nights. Evaluative feedback may be solicited from the participants after each of the instructional episodes. At the very minimum participants should be asked to provide evaluative feedback three or four times during the course.

The evaluation of instructional episodes need not be long, drawn-out affairs. Learners can be allowed three or four minutes at the end of each instructional episode to complete a checklist

70

or offer brief written comments about the instructional episode. Some teachers budget the last five minutes of class time for a general discussion; during the discussion the learners indicate what they liked and did not like about the instructional episode. Tests may sometimes be administered, but it should be announced that the tests are not for the purposes of grading. The test results simple indicate whether the educational objectives have been realized. Learners should not be asked to sign their names to tests.

A Model Instructional Plan

The following instructional plan will illustrate the concepts discussed in the foregoing paragraphs.

Teacher: John Smith

Date: December 4, 1976

Course: "Christians in the Modern World"

Instructional Plan: No. 8

1. Need/interest

The participants have determined that they need to know more about the social responsibilities of Christians today.

2. Topical question

What are some of the social responsibilities of Christians today?

3. Objective

At the conclusion of the instructional episode the participants will be able to identify at least four major social responsibilities of Christians today. (or) At the conclusion of the instructional episode the participants will understand some of the major social responsibilities of Christians today.

4. Resources

A. The participants
B. The instructor

C. The resource person
D. A filmstrip: "Christians in Today's World"

5. Techniques

A. Lecture (the instructor)
B. Filmstrip
C. Buzz session in small groups
D. Questions and answers (resource person)

6. Activity Outline

A. Introductory lecture (the instructor).....................10 minutes
B. Filmstrip...15 minutes
C. Buzz sessions...25 minutes
D. Questions and answers ....20 minutes
E. Concluding summary (instructor)........................10 minutes
F. Evaluation..10 minutes

7. Evaluation

At the conclusion of the instructional episode the participants will be asked to complete a brief written paragraph indicating the strengths and limitations of the educational activities.

Conclusion

Instructional planning assists the teacher to impose boundaries upon adult learning activities. An instructional plan serves as a handy guideline for the teacher. It is also helpful for the learners. At the beginning of each instructional episode the teacher may wish to distribute copies of the instructional plan to the learners, thus enabling them to preview what will take place.

A word of caution: instructional plans are highly useful, but they should not be perceived as something carved in stone. There are times when the teacher and learners will want to forsake the instructional plan for the sake of serendipity: the unplanned and fortuitous occurrence of a good thing. If adult learners are enthuasiastic and excited about an idea, it serves no good purpose to move on to another idea simply because the instructional plan calls for such a movement. Instructional plans should be our servants, not our masters.

Instructional plans should be our servants, not our masters.

9. Planning Workshops: Avoiding Spongeshops

Busy adults generally find the workshop approach to adult education more attractive than ongoing courses that are conducted, say, once a week for several weeks. People are usually able to set aside a weekend for attendance at a workshop but are reluctant to enroll in courses that require attendance over a longer period of time.

A workshop consists of a series of interrelated events or learning activities that are directed toward a single theme or problem. Some workshops last only a day; other workshops may be of three or four days duration. The greatest problem facing workshop organizers, I suggest, does not concern promotion of the workshop, scheduling, contracting the services of speakers, or any of the other important tasks associated with workshop design. The most crucial question confronting workshop coordinators concerns the active involvement of the participants in the workshop events.

Spongeshops

The overwhelming number of workshops I have attended have been advertised as workshops when, in fact, they were little more than spongeshops. A spongeshop consists of a series of back-to-back lectures. A number of experts are invited to make speeches or read papers. The participants are invited to play the role of sponges: they are asked to soak up the information presented to them by the speakers. The most vigorous activity undertaken by participants at spongeshops is either taking notes at a furious pace or fooling around with tape recorders.

Most persons responsible for conducting workshops, in my experience at least, have not the faintest idea of the workshop approach to education. This is true of workshop coordinators in all areas of life: government, the professional field of education, community service agencies, etc. The people who are least effective in conducting workshops, again in my experience, are people in business and in religious education. Businessmen and industrialists, together with religious educators, need quite a bit of help in organizing the workshop experience. But I digress.

What happens at the typical spongeshop violates nearly every important principle of adult education. The spongeshop situation is teacher-dominated instead of participatory; passivity is expected of the participants instead of activity; the rich and varied life experiences of the participants are never tapped;

The overwhelming number of workshops I have attended have been advertised as workshops when, in fact, they were little more than spongeshops.

shared monologues deny the possibility of participant dialogues; adult education is visualized very narrowly as the imparting of information data. This narrow conceptualization of adult education goes hand-in-hand with the less admirable trait, exhibited by some visiting experts, of vainglory. I often wonder how many visiting experts have used the workshop format for the purposes of taking an ego trip. Some visiting experts mount the platform, deliver their speeches authoritatively, and bask in the adulation of the non-experts who soak up what is said. Both a misconception of adult education and human pride sometimes turn occasions of possible growth into less than satisfying experiences.

Make no mistake, the lecture technique in itself is a good technique. But too much of a good thing makes for boredom. The overuse of the lecture technique implies that the learners have little to contribute to the learning process and that they are, after all, mere empty vessels into which knowledge is to be poured. The overuse of the lecture technique in adult religious education, it may be speculated, is due to the "pulpit effect" on religious education. People who are exposed Sunday after Sunday to someone transmitting information to them from the pulpit find it natural to use, and overuse, this technique in educational situations in general and at workshops in particular.

Four Techniques

There are ways to enliven workshops and stimulate the active participation of people in the learning process. There are ways to insure that workshops do not degenerate into spongeshops. In this chapter I shall describe four techniques for involving participants in workshop activities. Each of these techniques, as will be seen, may be employed in a variety of ways. Planners and coordinators of workshops may wish to incorporate some of these techniques into the next workshop they design.

1. Group discussion

A discussion group is composed of eight to 14 members who are given at least 45 minutes to address themselves to a topic, theme, or problem. The discussion group ordinarily has a designated leader; it is the goal of the leader to keep watch on the discussion process. The leader strives to create an environment where individual participation in the discussion is balanced.

The discussion group technique, as well as the other techniques described below, may be used **proactively** or **reactively.**

In this chapter I shall describe four techniques for involving participants in workshop activities.

The proactive discussion group initiates considerations of a particular theme and generates questions which are to be answered by a visiting expert or resource person.

The reactive discussion group meets after a visiting expert has delivered a lecture, or after the workshop participants have viewed a film, for example. The group reacts to what group members heard and saw. Generally the reactive discussion group issues a report which evaluates the ideas that have been presented via a lecture, film, or some other process.

An example. Approximately 50 people gather for a one-day workshop. The facilitator asks the people to divide into groups of ten. He assigns the same task to each group: make a list of questions to be addressed to the visiting expert. In completing this task the groups will be functioning as proactive discussion groups.

Suppose the visiting expert first delivers a speech. The participants divide into discussion groups and talk about the ideas expressed in the speech; they evaluate these ideas and prepare a summary report. The summary report is shared with all of the workshop participants at a general session. In this case the discussion group is a reactive group.

2. Buzz groups

Buzz groups have fewer members than a discussion group (anywhere from three to seven) and spend much less time in dialogue than do discussion groups. A typical buzz group may meet for only ten or 15 minutes. Buzz groups may also be used as proactive or reactive groups. The use of buzz groups is advised when the workshop schedule is crowded and the time constraints are great.

Another example. The workshop lecturer poses a problem and alternative answers to the problem. He wants feedback from the participants before he goes on to present his response to the problem. The lecturer asks the participants to divide into groups of five. The task of the buzz groups is to select one of the alternative answers to the problem. After 15 minutes the lecturer asks for a brief statement from each of the buzz groups describing how the problem should be handled. After he has heard from each group, the lecturer proceeds to examine the various responses of the buzz groups and to present his own solutions to the problem.

3. Panel

There are usually four, five, or six persons on a panel. Panel members discuss given issues while the participants and visiting expert observe the discussion. Panel discussion may last from 30 to 45 minutes. After the panel discussion has been completed, the visiting expert may respond to the discussion and/or other workshop participants may ask questions of the panelists. Panels may also be employed reactively, e.g., to react to what has been presented in a lecture.

An example will clarify how panels may be used. In a workshop of 50 persons the visiting expert presents a lecture. After the lecture the participants divide into groups of ten and conduct discussions of the lecture. At the conclusion of the discussion session one member from each group is selected to serve as a panelist. The panelists report on what took place in their discussion groups and discuss the issues further. The expert and other participants listen and observe. After the panel has finished its task, the expert or resource person responds to the ideas that emerged from the panel discussion; other participants are given the opportunity of reacting to what the panelists said.

4. Multiplying dyads

One of the most effective approaches for involving workshop participants is the multiplying dyad technique. A dyad is a group of two persons. Two persons meet for three or four minutes for a brief discussion of some issue. On the word of the facilitator the dyads pair, e.g., two dyads join together for another brief discussion. After seven or eight minutes the facilitator asks each group of four to join another group of four. The groups of eight (or nine or ten depending on the number of persons "left over" after pairing) meet for ten or 15 minutes. Multiplying dyads offers opportunities for everyone in a workshop to say something and exchange ideas.

Multiplying dyads offers opportunities for everyone in a workshop to say something and to exchange ideas.

Here is an example of the use of multiplying dyads. The workshop facilitator shows a film and asks the participants to react to the film by evaluating and commenting on its content. He asks the participants to divide into dyads. (If there is an uneven number of people, one group will have three persons.) For three or four minutes the participants talk to each other about the film. The facilitator asks each dyad to join another dyad. In groups of four the participants comment on the film. After six or seven minutes the facilitator asks the groups of four to form groups of eight. The participants continue to react to the film for about 15 minutes. One of the participants, from each of the groups of eight, summarizes the group discussion and reports to the entire workshop. A visiting expert may react to the reports.

Variations

It is obvious from the examples above that each of the four techniques outlined in this article may be used in conjunction with lecture and film techniques, and in combination with each other. The use of several techniques in a workshop brings much variation to workshop activities. Buzz sessions may lead to a panel discussion; a panel discussion may provide issues to be discussed by multiplying dyads; group discussion may generate issues to which the source person responds; a lecture may lead to a panel discussion which, in turn, may lead to reactive multiplying dyads, and so forth.

A Model Program

To illustrate how the four techniques may be employed, the following workshop schedule is offered as a model.

Here is the scenario: Forty-three religion teachers from a particular community are meeting for a one-day workshop. The workshop is ecumenical and will concern some of the major educational problems of the teachers. A visiting expert, Mary Smith, will be present for the workshop. She has several years teaching experience and holds an advanced degree in religious education. The workshop facilitator is Mr. Brown, director of religious education for the church hosting the workshop.

9:00 AM—Registration

The participants register for the workshop from 9:00 to 9:30. During the 30 minutes the facilitator introduces himself to the participants and informally introduces the participants to one another. Since they will be collaborating with each other on common problems, workshop participants should make some effort to know one another.

9:30 AM—Welcome (Mr. Brown)

The facilitator briefly welcomes the participants to the workshop and makes any announcements that are necessary. Some "housekeeping" chores are inevitable at every workshop and they should be addressed immediately. The facilitator then introduces Mary Smith to the workshop participants.

9:45 AM—Opening Lecture (Mary Smith)

Mary Smith speaks for approximately 30 minutes. She introduces the general topic of the workshop, makes an initial statement vis-a-vis the topic, offers a few suggestions for the teachers, and raises some questions for discussion.

10:15 AM—Group Discussions

The facilitator asks the participants to divide into groups of ten (approximately). In each group there will be a designated leader who will later become a member of a panel. The groups are given 45 minutes to react to Mary Smith's lecture. Members of the groups will examine and evaluate Mary Smith's suggestions, and will respond to some of the questions she has raised.

11:00 AM—Panel Discussion

The leaders of the discussion groups become members of a panel. They report the main ideas expressed in the groups and add their individual commentaries. The panel discussion continues for 45 minutes.

11:45 AM—Response (Mary Smith)

Mary Smith responds briefly to the issues and questions discussed by the panelists.

The facilitator announces that the lunch hour will last from 12:00 to 1:00 p.m.

1:00 PM—Filmstrip and Commentary (Mary Smith)

Mary Smith introduces an appropriate filmstrip for the teachers and adds a short commentary after the filmstrip has been shown. The filmstrip and commentary lasts roughly 45 minutes.

1:45 PM—Buzz Groups

The facilitator asks the participants to divide into groups of four or five. The task of the buzz groups is to react to the filmstrip and commentary. The buzz groups meet for 15 minutes.

2:00 PM—Reports from the Buzz Groups

A reporter from each buzz group makes a brief report concerning the discussion in his/her buzz group.

2:30 PM—Response (Mary Smith)

Mary Smith responds to the statements issued by the buzz group reporters.

3:00 PM—Multiplying Dyads

The facilitator asks the participants to form pairs. (Since there are 43 participants, one of the group will have three members.) The participants are to identify some of the problems that confront them as teachers. After three or four minutes the facilitator asks the dyads to pair. Participants will continue to discuss the same topic. After six or seven minutes the facilitator asks the participants to form groups of eight or nine. The same topic is addressed. The groups of eight will review the content of the dyadic and paired dyadic discussions; the groups of eight will be allotted 15 minutes to continue the discussion. One member from each group will be responsible for summarizing and reporting the discussion.

3:45 PM—Reports from Groups

The reporter from each group of eight shares with all of the participants the ideas expressed in the group. Several problems will have been identified.

4:15 PM—Response (Mary Smith)

Mary Smith attempts to answer some of the problems raised by the participants.

4:45 PM—Final Remarks (Mr. Brown)

The facilitator distributes paper and pencils to the participants and asks for their comments concerning the workshop. After the evaluation has taken place, the facilitator collects the papers, thanks the participants for attending, and brings closure.

Conclusion

It will be noted that the employment of the involvement techniques has created a situation in which participants are in active pursuit of knowledge and skills, a situation that invites input from the participants, a situation that fosters communication among the workshop participants and dialogue between the visiting expert and the participants.

It is not necessary, of course, to employ all four of the techniques in every workshop. Four involvement techniques were used in the model one-day workshop for sake of illustration.

Adult educators and workshop organizers can do much to help adults learn within the workshop format. Effective learning will take place, it is suggested, only when the participants are actively involved in the workshop proceedings. Those who are responsible for the organization and implementation of workshops, at all costs, must initiate strategies that prevent the transformation of workshops into spongeshops.

10. Planning for Evaluation

Religious educators who deal with adult learners should be particularly interested in educational evaluation. Programs in which learners voluntarily participate must be continually improved in terms of the educational enrichment accruing to participants and in terms of participant satisfaction. This ongoing improvement of education is accomplished principally through evaluation.

In this chapter I shall address some general questions about educational evaluation, indicate different levels at which evaluation may take place, and offer some suggestions on the procedures involved in educational evaluation.

What is evaluation?

Evaluation is the judgment of the worth of an educational program, course, or episode. This judgment is based on collected data and on an analysis of the data and observations. Evaluation is not simply guesswork about the effectiveness of education; it is not a vague apprehension or intuition that something is successful or unsuccessful. Evaluative judgments must be rational, which is to say evaluative judgment must be based on evidence.

Evaluative judgments must be rational, which is to say evaluative judgment must be based on evidence.

Why evaluate?

One of the main rationales for educational evaluation is the improvement of education. The motto of General Electric must apply to education also: "Progress is our most important product." In the evaluation process both the strengths and the weaknesses of a program are identified. What is good in a program should be underscored for future emphasis; what is dysfunctional should be negated, minimized, or regulated.

Who collects data?

The evaluative judgment is based on collected data. In the context of a local church or parish those who are responsible for the implementation of the program (director of religious education, adult education council, leaders and teachers) may

82

collect the data. If a local church or parish can afford the services of an evaluation consultant, the consultant should be hired. Sometimes an outside consultant brings more objectivity into the evaluation process . A professional consultant will also assist in developing an evaluation design specifically for the situation. Furthermore, an outside consultant may be able to untangle some of the complexities involved in educational evaluation.

In those places where it would be unrealistic to contract the services of an expert, the evaluation should be carried out by those who are responsible for the program. An evaluation that is conducted by non-experts is better than no evaluation at all.

What is the source of data?

Evaluation of an adult program should be based largely on data collected from participants in the program. Participants should be asked what they liked about the program and what they disliked. They should be asked to pass judgments on the program (the judgments of participants become the data on which the evaluators base their judgments). Participants should also be given the opportunity of stating whether they learned anything through participation in the program; they should be invited to suggest ways for program improvement.

Data collection should avoid as much as possible the administration of school-type tests (to assess how well objectives were met) to adult learners. The ideal is to make data collecting unobtrusive so that adult learners will not get the idea they are being judged or compared.

Attendance records should be kept and increased or decreased attendance during the program should be analysed in terms of what was happening in the program. When adults are alienated from an educational program, they vote with their feet; they simply refuse to attend learning sessions. Sometimes declining attendance in a program may be correlated with program characteristics.

The data collector should seek input from those who dropped out of the program. Examination of "dropout" attitudes toward the program is just as important as analysis of participant attitudes.

In many ways the evaluation of an adult program is easier than the evaluation of a program for children. Adults generally have judgmental competencies not possessed by children. Adults can be more fully involved in the evaluation process by supplying to the data collector judgments which relate to program effectiveness.

Examination of "dropout" attitudes toward the program is just as important as analysis of participant attitudes.

How is data collected?

There are many different ways to collect data. A few of the more effective ways are: 1) observation of the program by the data collector, 2) surveys administered to program participants, and 3) interviews of selected participants and "drop outs."

The data collector should observe what is happening in the program and keep a log or diary which reports on observed events. In other words, the process of collecting evaluative data is coterminous with the program. During the program, from beginning to end, observations may be taken and noted in writing. It is not necessary, in other words, to wait until the conclusion of the program to begin collecting data.

The participants may be asked to respond to a questionnaire which includes a variety of questions about the program, about their attitudes toward the program, and about specific elements in the program.

The data collector may wish to interview randomly selected participants to gain a more detailed understanding of participant reaction. Surveys and questionnaires are helpful in collecting a wide variety of participant reactions but the interview technique provides a more in-depth understanding of participant reactions. Those who enrolled in the program and subsequently "dropped out" should also be contacted and interviewed. It is the task of the data collector to locate precisely the source of dissatisfaction (if any) with a program on the part of those who stopped attending.

Who passes judgments?

After data has been collected, the time comes to pass judgments about the worth of the program. It is suggested that the entire adult education council review the data and make judgments about the program. These judgments, together with suggestions for the improvement of future programs, should be in written form. The evaluation reports from one evaluation to the next should be kept on file and should be reviewed occasionally. This helps the adult education council to plot out the patterns of program improvement that have taken place.

What elements are evaluated?

Any educational program has an almost infinite number of elements that could possibly be evaluated. I suggest that evaluations focus on eight of these elements: 1) program objectives, 2) context, 3) content, 4) methods, 5) techniques, 6) transactions, 7) resources, and 8) relationship between objectives and outcomes.

Again, an almost infinite number of questions may be asked about each of the elements in an educational program. The following questions may be asked:

Objectives:

1. Have the program objectives been written out prior to program implementation? (If the objectives have not been written out in advance of the program, the evaluation process will not uncover some highly pertinent data.)
2. Are the objectives clearly stated?
3. Are the objectives realistic and attainable?
4. Are the objectives stated in such a way that the evaluators will be able to determine if they have been accomplished? (All too often educational objectives are expressed in glittering generalities, e.g., the objective of the program is to become better Christians.)
5. Were objectives formulated in terms of assessed learner needs? and interests?

Context:

1. What is the reaction of the participants to the places where they met? Comfortable? Well-lighted? Convenient to reach? Roomy? Quiet?
2. What is the reaction of the participants to the times scheduled for educational activities?

Content:

1. What is the reaction of the participants to the subject matter or content of the program? Did the subject matter satisfy the needs and interests of the participants? Did the content of the program facilitate or impede the attainment of the objectives?

Methods:

1. What is the reaction of the participants to the methods employed in the program (class sessions, workshops, correspondence study, group discussion)?
2. Could program objectives be reached more efficiently through different methods?

Techniques:

1. What is the reaction of the participants to the techniques employed in the program (use of films, panels, lectures, etc.)?
2. Were a sufficient variety of techniques used?

Transactions:

1. Did the leaders/teachers get along well with the learners?
2. Did the participants get along well with one another?

Resources:

1. What is the reaction of the participants to the human resources employed in the program, e.g., guest speakers?

2. What is the reaction of the participants to the material resources used in the program (books, films, duplicated materials, etc.)?

Outcomes:

1. What are the outcomes of the program?
2. What are the discrepancies between objectives and outcomes?
3. How can these discrepancies be explained?
4. What outcomes occurred that were not anticipated?
5. How can favorable unanticipated outcomes be incorporated into the program?
6. How can unfavorable unanticipated outcomes be negated?

It is not necessary to answer all of the previous questions in program evaluation. The **scope** of the evaluation may be broad and treat many different elements in the program or it may be narrow and deal with selected elements. Those who are responsible for the program should determine the scope of the program evaluation. A word of caution: it is probably better to narrow the scope of the program evaluation the first few times programs are evaluated. As the evaluators gain expertise through the experience of program evaluation, they may wish to broaden the scope of evaluations gradually. This word of caution is offered because some beginning evaluators "bite off more than they can chew" the first few times they evaluate programs.

The following sample questionnaire represents an attempt to gain evaluative data for an evaluation that is somewhat narrow in scope. The quesionnaire could be used the first time the program is evaluated and expanded for future evaluations.

Sample Evaluation Questionnaire

We are presently evaluating the Fall adult education program. We want to improve the program for next Spring on the basis of our evaluation. Will you please take a few moments to complete this questionnaire?

Many thanks for your help.

The Adult Education Council

Please state the course(s) you attended.

Circle your response to each of the following items.

1. I learned very much from the program.

Strongly   Strongly
agree   Agree   Uncertain   Disagree   disagree

2. The subject matter of the program was **not** interesting.

Strongly   Strongly
agree   Agree   Uncertain   Disagree   disagree

3. The physical surroundings were comfortable.

Strongly   Strongly
agree   agree   Uncertain   Disagree   disagree

4. A sufficient number of educational techniques were employed.

Strongly   Strongly
agree   Agree   Uncertain   Disagree   disagree

5. Meetings were **not** scheduled at a convenient time.

Strongly   Strongly
agree   Agree   Uncertain   Disagree   disagree

6. The texts were interesting and adequate.

Strongly   Strongly
agree   Agree   Uncertain   Disagree   disagree

7. The teacher was **not** friendly.

Strongly   Strongly
agree   Agree   Uncertain   Disagree   disagree

8. All of the participants got along together very well.

Strongly   Strongly
agree   Agree   Uncertain   Disagree   disagree

9. I did **not** have much of an opportunity to participate actively.

Strongly   Strongly
agree   Agree   Uncertain   Disagree   disagree

10. I intend to participate in the next program.

Strongly   Strongly
agree   Agree   Uncertain   Disagree   disagree

Please respond briefly to the following questions.

11. What did you like most about the program?

12. What did you like least about the program?

13. What topics should be treated in the next program?

14. How can our adult education program be improved?

Levels of Evaluation

Reference has been made previously to programs, course, and episode. It will be remembered that a series of educational episodes makes up a course; a series of courses makes up a total program. This distinction brings forward the notion of different levels of evaluation. A total program may be evaluated, a course may be evaluated, and/or an educational episode may be evaluated.

In evaluating an educational episode the teacher will ask the participants to fill out a very brief questionnaire, conduct a brief evaluative discussion, take a test (if there is no other way to gather data), or jot down some evaluative judgments about the episode. Suppose a course is made up of seven episodes. If the teacher conducts a post-session evaluation for three or four of these episodes, he will gather data that may be used in the evaluation of the course. Similarly, if course evaluations are conducted at the conclusion of each course, the data collected by the teacher may be used in the evaluation of the total program.

Evaluation at all three levels should be encouraged. Teachers should be asked to evaluate educational episodes occasionally and should be permitted to devise their own questionnaires to collect evaluative data at the conclusion of the courses they teach. In some cases a **program** evaluation may legitimately be made on the basis of evaluative data regarding educational episodes and courses. In other cases the adult education council may wish to prepare a questionnaire to obtain additional data about the total program.

It may seem that I am suggesting too much time be given to evaluation. If we really believe, however, that our programs can be improved, we will not be unenthusiastic about gathering the data necessary for program improvement. Evaluation is emphasized, also, because it is not common to find evaluation practiced systematically in educational programs sponsored by parishes and local churches. Too often evaluative judgments are snap judgments based on general feelings about a program.

Too often evaluative judgements are snap judgments based on general feelings about a program.

Evaluation: A Model

Perhaps the best way to conclude this brief chapter is to offer a framework or model for conducting program evaluation. The following procedure may be of some help to those who wish to assess the worth of their educational programs.

1. Identify elements of the program that are to be evaluated.
2. Formulate evaluative questions.
3. Determine ways of collecting data.
4. Collect data.
5. Study data.
6. Render evaluative judgments.
7. Report summary of data and judgments.

Program elements. It has been indicated above that every educational program contains an almost infinite number of elements that are amenable to evaluation. The first task of the evaluators is to focus on a selected number of these elements. Suppose, for instance, an adult education council decides to evaluate the program objectives, the space-time context of the program, the techniques that were used, the material resources, and the relationship between objectives and outcomes. The decision to limit the evaluation to these five elements represents a scoping tactic and defines the boundaries of the evaluation process.

Evaluative questions. Proceeding to the second step in the model the adult education council will develop questions concerning each of the five elements they have selected. For example, questions under the heading of "objectives" may be:

1. Do program objectives meet the needs and interests of the learners?
2. Are the program objectives realistic and attainable?
3. Did the learners know the objectives of each course before the course began?
4. Were the objectives stated clearly?

Ways of collecting data. After questions for each of the program elements have been formulated, the adult education council must determine how data will be collected. **Since evaluation planning takes place before program implementation, it is possible to identify a number of ways of collecting data during the program as well as after the program has been completed. The adult education council may wish to devise a questionnaire to be administered after the program, arrange for the observation of the program by the director of religious education during the program, list a number of questions that may be used for interviewing "drop outs," and so forth.**

Collection of data. As has been noted in the foregoing paragraph, data may be collected by the religious education director, teachers, and others during the program; data is also collected at the conclusion of the program.

Study data. Once the data from observations, interviews, questionnaires, and other techniques have been organized in summary form, the adult education council studies the data to prepare for the rendering of evaluative judgments.

Render judgments. On the basis of the examined data the adult education council makes judgments about the program and determines ways of improving future programs.

Report. A summary of the data together with the evaluative judgments of the adult education council and the council's recommendations for future improvements is prepared and filed. Records of evaluations are kept to maintain administrative continuity between one program and succeeding programs. When new members take their places on the adult education council, they should be encouraged to brief themselves by referring to past records of evaluations.

Conclusion

No doubt some people assume educational programs are worthwhile merely because they are religious education programs. This is unfortunate since no educational effort of the local church or parish can survive over the long haul without some kind of evaluation. If religious educators fail to evaluate their programs they risk spending time, energy, and money traveling in a direction that leads to educational oblivion. Educational evaluation may itself be time consuming, energy consuming, and at times, costly, but in the absence of educational evaluation progress cannot be an important product of religious educators.

No doubt some people assume educational programs are worthwhile merely because they are religious education programs. This is unfortunate since no educational effort of the local church or parish can survive over the long haul without some kind of evaluation.

11. Organizing Discussion Groups (I)

Adult education in the parish or local church frequently takes place in the discussion group. Small groups of adults meet on a regular basis and discuss ideas and issues that are either assigned or selected by the adults themselves. The discussion group method has been in vogue for many years and it would appear that little could be said about the method that would be new. Directors of religious education have probably gained much experience with discussion groups and may possibly feel that organizing a discussion group is a simple matter. The organization and management of an effective discussion group, however, is a complex task that requires more than a little expertise.

In this chapter I shall consider some of the processes involved in organizing an effective discussion group: 1) the organization of the discussion content or subject matter, 2) the organization of roles in the discussion group, and 3) the installation of norms that facilitate effective group discussion. I have borrowed ideas liberally from the Bergevin and McKinley book *Participation Training for Adult Education*[1]—a little book that has helped literally thousands of adult learners develop results-oriented discussion groups. "Participation Training" is a designation for a specific type of adult learning group. To some extent I have modified the ideas offered by Bergevin and McKinley in preparing this chapter. It would not be a waste of time for the reader of this chapter to examine *Participation Training for Adult Education* and compare its contents with the concepts presented in this chapter.

Organizing Discussion Content

On one occasion I participated in a group discussion with a number of other persons who were educational consultants. We were invited by a national organization to pool our insights in

[1] Bergevin, Paul and McKinley, John, *Participation Training for Adult Education,* St. Louis: Bethany Press, 1965.

hopes of establishing fresh guidelines for organization development. For the better part of a day ten of us sat around a table conducting a discussion that was "all over the ball park." Finally one of the group members addressed himself to the executives who convened the meeting. "I'd feel a whole lot better about my place in the discussion," he said, "if I knew what topic we were discussing."

It may sound peculiar, but we conducted a discussion for several hours without a discussion topic. We talked about everything and, therefore, talked about nothing. We were not really members of a group communicating **with** one another; we were individuals making little speeches **at** one another. Eventually the group selected a specific topic and succeeded in exploring at least one issue in some depth.

Many group discussions begin without a specific topic, or with a topic that is formulated badly and imprecisely. As a consequence, members of the group interpret the meaning of the topic differently and begin to converse at cross purposes. "Christian Social Responsibilities" as a topic, for example, is open to many different interpretations. One person may wish to talk about the scriptural evidence that mandates Christians to be socially responsible, another person may wish to talk about the social responsibilities of the institutional Church, still another person may want to discuss the history of Christian social responsiveness. If the topic is not formulated adequately, it can be, in effect, many topics.

In formulating a discussion topic, the topic should be framed in terms of a question that cannot be answered by a "yes" or a "no." The question format for the topic is suggested because interrogative formulations stimulate inquiry among the learners. When questions are answerable by a "yes" or a "no," what usually happens is that the discussion degenerates into a debate or never gets off the ground.

Example:

TOPIC—Do Christians have social responsibilities? If some of the group members respond affirmatively and others answer "no," the group will be split into "sides" and a debate will take place instead of a group search for knowledge, wisdom, and meaning. If everyone agrees that Christians do have social responsibilities, no discussion is possible. The group merely answers "yes" and adjourns.

A more suitable formulation of the topic would be "What are the social responsibilities of Christians?" or "Why do Christians have social responsibilities?" (The questions are not, by the way, loaded. A group could conceivably decide that there are no social responsibilities of Christians or that there are no cogent reasons why Christians have social responsibilities.) A handy rule of thumb: questions that begin with "why," "how," "what," and "when" usually result in adequately formulated topics; questions that begin with "should" and "do" ordinarily result in topical questions for debate.

A topic could be formulated meeting the requirements stated above and still not be a meaningful topical question. Topical questions should also be focused.

Here is an example of an unfocused topical question:

TOPIC—What are the social responsibilities of Christians?

Here is an example of a focused topical question:

TOPIC—What are four important social responsibilities we have as Christians?

An unfocused topical question leads to the exchange of sparkling generalities; a focused topical question puts boundaries around the issue to be discussed and identifies a road that is to be traveled by the discussion group. In asking for four important social responsibilities, the focused topic in the example delineates precisely the direction that is to be taken by the group. The example of the focused topic also "brings the discussion home." The topic asks for social responsibilities that **we** have as Christians. As such the topic addresses itself to the actual lives of those who are members of the discussion group.

At the beginning of this chapter I mentioned that topics are sometimes assigned to groups. This practice should be avoided on grounds that are highly practical: groups that discuss assigned topics typically find that the discussion breaks down. On the other hand, people are enthusiastic about discussing topics they have chosen. The reason for this may be stated in terms of **commitment.** There is usually a high degree of group commitment to topics selected by discussion groups; this degree of commitment is ordinarily lacking when groups are presented with a topic by someone outside of the group.

If discussion groups correctly formulated a topical question, this practice would itself facilitate discussion. But the content of group discussion can be organized even further by stating a goal. Research on group work has shown that the cohesive group is the group whose members share the same goal.

The goal of every group discussion is contained in the topical question. It is necessary, however, to make the goal quite explicit.

TOPIC—What are four important social responsibilities we have as Christians?

There is usually a high degree of group commitment to topics selected by discussion groups; this degree of commitment is ordinarily lacking when groups are presented with a topic by someone outside of the group.

GOAL—To discuss four important social responsibilities we have as Christians.

Is the goal stated properly? No. As it stands the goal statement is really a statement of the **task** that is to be accomplished **during** the discussion and not what will result as a consequence or end-result of the discussion. The following statement of goal is more adequate:

GOAL—At the conclusion of the discussion session we shall have listed four important social responsibilities we have as Christians.

It must be remembered in formulating statements of goals that "goal" means "end-result" and not the task or tasks that are to take place during the discussion. Should not the discussion group state its tasks when planning the discussion? Yes. And this leads us to a consideration of the outline.

The discussion outline itemizes the tasks that will be accomplished by the group in order to reach the goal or goals. Here is an example:

TOPIC—What are four important social responsibilities we have as Christians?

GOAL—At the conclusion of the discussion session we shall have listed four important social responsibilities we have as Christians.

OUTLINE—
1. Brainstorming (tossing out ideas rapidly without evaluating them).
2. Making a list of a number of social responsibilities.
3. Arranging the list in a hierarchical order.
4. Selecting four social responsibilities that concern us in our specific situation.

By using topic, goal, and outline, the group members will have erected a structure or framework within which the discussion will take place. It may take time and practice to organize the discussion content, and the planning of the discussion may take longer than the discussion, but such planning is absolutely necessary for effective group discussion. In the long run less time will be wasted and more people will be satisfied with the group discussion.

The topic, goal, and outline—during the process of formulation and after they have been formulated—should be displayed on the chalkboard or on butcher paper so that all of the group members know exactly what is expected of them as group members. This serves also to remind group members of the topic, goal, and outline. It is very easy at times to forget the topic, goal, and outline in the midst of an interesting discussion. When the topic, goal, and outline are displayed in full view, group members may refer to the display to refresh their memories.

Organizing Discussion Roles

Content or subject matter is only one aspect of a discussion group. Each of the members of the group must also take roles in the discussion. These roles must be organized. The roles are: 1) participants, 2) moderator, 3) recorder, 4) resource person, and 5) evaluator. Specific functions or tasks are associated with each role.

Participants

The role of participant is most important. Most of the members of any discussion group will perform this role. Unfortunately, participants in discussion groups do not see themselves operating out of any special role. They merely join in the discussion without consciousness of specific tasks or functions required of them.

The following functions should be performed by group participants:

1. preparing for the discussion session by reading and/or thinking about the topic,

2. formulating the discussion topic, goal, and outline,

3. assisting others in the group to take part in the discussion,

4. helping others in the group to communicate by clarifying the statements of other members,

5. keeping the discussion on the topic,

6. listening politely and actively,

7. building on the statements of others in the group,

8. resolving conflicts among others in the group,

9. assisting the recorder in transcribing the flow of the discussion, and

10. discussing the evaluator's report after the discussion.

A number of other functions are related to the participant role; the functions listed above, I suggest, are the most important.

Moderator

The moderator of the group discussion has a role that is similar to the role enacted by the chairman or chairwoman at a meeting. The moderator is concerned with the regulation of intra-group discussion. Discussion groups should operate with different persons in the position of moderator at different times, e.g., the roles of moderator and recorder should not be filled on a permanent basis.

Here are some of the functions required of the group moderator:

1. initiating the discussion by introducing topic, goal, and outline,

2. keeping the discussion going purposefully,

3. bringing out all sides of an issue,

4. giving summaries of the discussion when needed,

5. helping to avoid domination by one or two of the members,

6. drawing all participants into the discussion,

7. inviting non-participating members into the discussion when they indicate by non-verbal cues that they wish to speak,

8. offering support to all of the members of the group,

9. helping the recorder transcribe the flow of the discussion, and

10. presenting a summary of the discussion and bringing closure (tying things up) at the end of the discussion.

Recorder

The recorder keeps track of the flow of the discussion by taking notes of the discussion. In essence the recorder serves as the memory of the group. The recorder should transcribe the flow of the discussion on a chalkboard or on butcher paper so that all of the participants may occasionally check on the stage of development of the discussion. The recorder helps the group members "stay on track."

Functions of the recorder include the following:

1. writing out the topic, goal, and outline,

2. writing out the main ideas expressed during the discussion,

3. writing out the main ideas in summary form,

4. writing out points of difference and agreement,

5. seeking help from the group when unsure of what to write, and

6. taking part in the discussion as a participant when convenient.

It should be noted that the recorder need not write out the names of participants who provide input into the discussion; the recorder is concerned only with the content of the discussion.

Resource Person

Occasionally a discussion group will invite a resource person to the discussion session. A resource person is someone who is particularly knowledgeable about a specific topic. Two extremes should be avoided in utilizing the services of a resource person: a) developing a state of over-dependency on the resource person and b) ignoring the presence of the resource person.

A typical failure of discussion groups vis-a-vis resource persons is the transformation of the discussion session into a "press conference." Sometimes the resource person or visiting expert is put into the role of the interviewee in a "Meet the Press" format. The discussion should be conducted as usual. When occasions arise that call for the input of the resource person, the resource person may be called upon to offer brief commentaries.

In avoiding an overdependency on the resource person the group members should not ignore the presence of the resource person. The resource person may be asked to make suggestions and provide information at various points during the discussion.

When an invitation is extended to the resource person, the resource person should be informed that he or she will not function as an expert at a press conference. Sometimes resource persons are disappointed when they are not permitted to "hold forth" during a group discussion. In other words, expectations should be reconciled and the terms of the resource person's participation in the group should be outlined when the invitation to participate is extended.

When an invitation is extended to a resource person, the resource person should be informed that he or she will not function as an expert at a press conference.

Evaluator

The evaluator is not an active participant during the discussion; the evaluator functions only after the discussion has been completed. The evaluator sits outside of the group where a more objective view of the group activities can be gained. At the conclusion of the discussion, the evaluator joins the group and gives a report concerning **group process.** The evaluation report, it must be emphasized, does not concern the content of the discussion.

Some people may think that the evaluator does not contribute anything important because of his or her non-participation during the discussion. This role, however, is extremely important. The use of the evaluator role can help discussion groups overcome bad habits of group process that may forestall group progress over a period of weeks or months.

The evaluator is not an analyst who attempts to understand the motivations underlying the behavior of group members; in the evaluation report the evaluator merely states his or her perceptions of overt behavior.

The following questions may be answered by the evaluator as the end-of-session report is being prepared. The evaluator should have a copy of these questions, and a pencil and pad to make notes during the discussion.

The evaluator is not an analyst who attempts to understand the motivations underlying the behavior of group members; in the evaluation report the evaluator merely states his or her perceptions of overt behavior.

Questions for the Evaluator

1. Was the participation of group members spontaneous?
2. Was there a balanced participation of all members?

3. What was the emotional climate like?

4. Did the group depend on the moderator too much? Too little?

5. What was the quality of listening?

6. How many interruptions took place?

7. How many times were the contributions of individual members overlooked?

8. Did members help one another communicate? How?

9. What are some examples of helpful behaviors that took place?

10. What are some examples of unhelpful behaviors that took place?

11. Did any members withdraw from the discussion or become overly passive?

12. How can the group process be improved for the next session?

After the discussion the evaluator discusses his responses to the above questions with the members of the discussion group. **The evaluator should not mention anyone by name.** If, for example, two members of the discussion group did most of the talking, the evaluator may say, "There was not a balanced participation in the discussion; there seemed to be evidence of domination by some of the members of the group."

The role of the evaluator can be performed on a permanent basis by someone who has had a measure of training in group processes, or it can be performed on a rotating basis by members of the discussion group.

Organization of discussion group roles is a difficult task. This is due chiefly to the fact that members of discussion groups are generally unaware of and inexperienced in the roles of moderator, recorder, evaluator, and participants. If roles are organized adequately, however, the discussion group members may learn something about group processes as well as something about the topics under discussion.

Installing Group Norms

Before a discussion group can become an effective learning system role functions must be carefully delineated and the subject matter of group discussions must be organized. These two items were treated in foregoing paragraphs. It is also necessary for members of the group to share norms of participation.

A norm is a principle or standard that governs and directs communication within the group. Five of these principles stand out as most important:

1. mutual acceptance,
2. willingness to listen,

3. willingness to share,
4. free, voluntary expression,
5. commitment to the task.

Mutual acceptance. Members of the discussion group must accept one another as persons and value the experiences and abilities of other members in the group. This does not mean that a member of a discussion group need feel constrained not to disagree with ideas that are brought up in the discussion. It does mean, however, that all disagreements will be offered in an agreeable manner. It means also that a mutual sense of respect pervades the relationships of the members of the group.

Willingness to listen. Each member of the group must be willing to listen to what other members of the group say. Seemingly this is simply a rule of politeness that should go without saying. Many groups, however, are characterized by much talking and little listening. All too often group members are busy formulating what they are going to say instead of paying close attention to what is said. Lacking a general willingness to listen on the part of group members spells defeat for the accomplishment of group goals. Willingness to listen, it may be noted, is an outgrowth of the first norm, mutual acceptance. When members of a group accept one another, effective listening takes place; lack of effective listening in a group is symptomatic of failure to abide by the norm of mutual acceptance.

Willingness to share. Members of a discussion group must be willing to share their ideas, opinions, insights, and experiences with the group. Each member of a discussion group is a repository of much experience, knowledge, and wisdom; the best resources for adult education are adults. It is not enough, then, that a group member become an effective listener. Group members must also become effective communicators.

Free, voluntary expression. Members of a discussion group should not be coerced into participating. In a discussion group adult learners should not be singled out or called upon by name in order to force participation. Very often such a tactic puts the learner "on the spot" and can be a source of embarrassment. In other words, participation in the discussion must be freely chosen. The norm of free, voluntary expression is balanced out by the norm of willingness to share. A sort of tension exists between these two norms. Each individual member of the group must deal with this tension in the best way available.

In a discussion group adult learners should not be singled out or called upon by name in order to force participation.

Commitment to the task. Members of a discussion group must be committed to the topic under discussion. Lack of enthusiasm or liking for the discussion topic sometimes creates long periods of silence in a group. The norm of commitment to task, therefore, is related to the ability of the group to select topics that have some degree of appeal for all of the members of the group.

How does a group facilitator install the above mentioned norms? First of all, members of the discussion group must be informed about the norms and what each of the norms means. They should be asked to give assent to the norms and to permit the norms to guide their interactions with others during group discussions.

When members of a discussion group first become aware of the norms, they usually give assent. The kind of assent they give, however, is what Cardinal Newman would call "notional" assent. They accept the norms in the abstract, but not necessarily in practice.

"Real" assent—assent in terms of behavior in the concrete order of reality—comes only through the process of group formation during the process of group discussion. The facilitator of a group will mention the norms frequently in order to remind discussion group members of the norms; the evaluator, in the post-session critique of the discussion, may wish to indicate the degree to which the norms were followed by the group. Over a period of time the norms will be transferred from group members' heads to group members' behaviors. "Real" assent to the norms comes only after practice and evaluation.

Conclusion

It was suggested at the head of this chapter that organizing discussion groups is a complex business. Some of the complexities involved in the organization process have been pointed out in the chapter. Another aspect of the organizational process—behaviors—will be discussed in the next chapter.

12. Organizing Discussion Groups (II)

Under careful analysis the apparently uncomplex discussion group is a highly complex system of interrelated components. We have already seen in the previous chapter that three of these major components are: 1) roles, 2) subject matter or content structure, and 3) norms. The fourth major component—one that will be discussed in this chapter—concerns behaviors. The following diagram of the "system" of discussion group components outlines their interrelatedness.

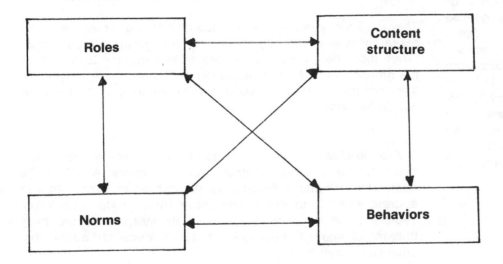

Components of a discussion group system

How the roles of moderator, recorder, resource person, participants, and evaluator are performed affects the content of discussion session, the operationalizing of the norms, and the behaviors of group members. The manner in which the discussion content is structured (topic, goal, outline) influences how roles are enacted, how closely the group members adhere to the norms, and how group members work during the discussion. Adherence to group norms relates to role performance, to the discussion content, and to individual behaviors of group members. The kinds of behaviors manifested by the group members determines, to some extent, how roles are performed, how subject matter is discussed, and how well norms are preserved.

Which of the four major components of a discussion group system is most important is not a question to be asked. All of the components are important. Special treatment is given to "behaviors" in this chapter simply because there is so much to say about behaviors that can take place during a discussion session.

In this chapter, then, I wish to outline several types of behavior that help or hinder group progress. The types of behaviors explained in this chapter have been identified by various researchers who have been concerned about the effectiveness of groups. Members of discussion groups who are sensitive to these behaviors, it is hoped, will be able to improve the quality of learning that takes place during group discussions.

What Not To Do: Dysfunctional Behaviors

There are many behaviors or kinds of behaviors discovered by researchers that are dysfunctional for group effectiveness. When these behaviors are manifested in groups, it is likely that the groups will find it difficult to reach their goals. Four types of behavior that must be avoided are: 1) dominating, 2) dropping out, 3) blocking, and 4) distracting.

There are many behaviors or kinds of behaviors discovered by researchers that are dysfunctional for group effectiveness. When these behaviors are manifested in groups, it is likely that the groups will find it difficult to reach their goals. Four types of behavior that must be avoided are: 1) dominating, 2) dropping out, 3) blocking, and 4) distracting.

The Dominator. The dominator usually talks a great deal much to the distress of other group members. At times the dominator exhibits a nervous quality which motivates him to address himself to every tiny issue in a group discussion. Typically, the dominator is a poor listener. He is too busy thinking of what he is going to say to be concerned about what others are saying.

The dominator does not stay on the topic of discussion very well; it takes little to move him away from the topic and off on a tangent. He is sometimes stubbornly insistent on the value of his ideas and becomes argumentative when his pet ideas or special interests are challenged. The more he talks, the less his input into the discussion is valued by other members of the group. The less his input is valued, the more he talks. He seems convinced that what is important is not the quality of ideas but the quantity of words.

Those in positions of authority must take special care they do not fall in into the role of dominator.

Those in positions of authority must take special care they do not fall into the role of dominator. It is quite easy for a pastor or a chairman of a church committee to misinterpret their responsibilities as authority figures and begin to see themselves as lecturers, instead of facilitators of group discussion.

The Dropout. Every member of a discussion group has a great store of experiences and sees the world from a specific point of view. His experience qualifies him as a responsible, mature, and informed individual. His view of the world is unique and irreplaceable.

It is the purpose of any problem-solving team to reach decisions on the basis of sharing experiences and points of view. When people share their experiences and points of view they bring into decision-making their combined resources, resources that permit the effective resolution of problems.

A dropout is a person who refuses to share his experience and point of view with others. As a result the group must complete its task while lacking a valuable resource.

The dropout usually pushes his chair back from the table, folds his arms, doodles on a piece of scratch paper, and engages in other activities that suggest his boredom or disgust.

What motivates a person to take the role of dropout is anybody's guess. Perhaps he would rather be somewhere else; perhaps he is not interested in the topic of discussion; perhaps he feels slighted or offended. Any number of anti-group feelings may motivate his behavior. (Sometimes people are physically ill and are unable to participate fully in the discussion. On these occasions people are not to be considered dropouts.)

The dropout's refusal to contribute to the group effort impoverishes the group and makes group learning very difficult.

The Blocker. Most discussion groups have specific goals to accomplish or tasks to complete. Blocking behavior is that behavior which places barriers between the group and group goals; it is behavior that interferes with the completion of the group task.

The blocker does not consistently control the pattern of discussion as does the dominator, but the blocker does insert irrelevant conversation at crucial points. Just as the group is ready to reach a decision, the blocker may take the flow of conversation off on a tangent. Just as the group is ready to complete its task, the blocker may raise a further, and often meaningless question.

Sometimes the blocker is not interested in solving a problem or completing a task; he merely enjoys group discussion and wants to prolong it to meet his individual needs for social intercourse.

At other times a group member will take the role of blocker to oppose indirectly a decision made by the group which he does not like. The blocker on occasion will subtly initiate a filibuster when the group is about to suggest a response to a problem that is not agreeable to the blocker.

Most blocking in group discussions occurs at an unconscious level.

Most blocking in group discussions occurs at an unconscious level. The blocker does not set out maliciously to forestall group endeavors. More often than not blocking behaviors are the result of carelessness, and thoughtlessness regarding group purpose.

The Distracter. Nothing impedes groups more than distraction. It is difficult enough for an individual to think about a problem rigorously and systematically; the thought processes of a group require much more discipline and concentration. Any kind of distracting influence such as outside noises and interruptions are likely to oppose systematic thinking in a group.

Again, the role of distracter is usually taken without malice or conscious design to undermine, the efforts of the group. But distracting behavior ordinarily exerts dysfunctional influences, on the group that are as powerful as the influences caused by dominators, dropouts, or blockers.

The distracter may tap his pencil on the table, gaze about the room, whisper to someone next to him, make clucking noises with his mouth, and generally makes a nuisance of himself.

In some cases the distracter is looking for attention from other members of the group. In most cases, however, the distracter's behavior may be attributed merely to a lack of concern for the sensitivities of others.

What To Do: Functional Behaviors

A constellation of functional behaviors has been uncovered by researchers. Functional behaviors may be described as those behaviors that help the group get its job done and/or behaviors that help maintain group spirit and cohesiveness. Five of these functional roles are: 1) builder, 2) gate keeper, 3) harmonizer, 4) encourager and, 5) clarifier.

Five functional roles are: 1) builder, 2) gate keeper, 3) harmonizer, 4) encourager, and 5) clarifier.

The Builder. In a discussion group it is necessary to maintain continuity and relationship among the ideas expressed by the members of the group. One of the ways of maintaining this continuity is by building upon the ideas of others.

When a member of the group says something, it is ordinarily productive for another member to "connect" what he says to what has been stated. Someone may contribute a particular approach to a given problem; the builder will accept this contribution and explore its ramifications. In other words, when a member of a group makes a statement, the statement should not be ignored. Other members of the group should try to construct ideas on foundation statements. When members of a group build upon the ideas of one another, problem solving becomes easier and tasks are accomplished more efficiently.

The Gate Keeper. At every meeting there may be one or two persons who are retiring, timid, and reticent about jumping into the discussion. At times these people give little non-verbal signals (throat clearing, hand raising, etc.) which indicate they would like to participate in the discussion. All too often these people are ignored by the other group members.

At times people give little non-verbal signals (throat clearing, hand raising, etc.) which indicate they would like to participate in the discussion. All too often these people are ignored by the other group members.

The function of the gate keeper is to be sensitive to others who may want to speak and to invite these persons into the discussion. The gate keeper will also keep track of persons who are interrupted and will ask them, at an appropriate time, to continue to speak at the point they were interrupted. "John was saying something a little while ago," a gate keeper might say, "and he never got a chance to finish his statement."

In many ways the role of gate keeper is the most important of the functional roles. A gate keeper in every group assures that the contributions of group members are not overlooked.

The Harmonizer. It is not unusual in every group that conflict, covert or overt, may be present. It is the task of the harmonizer to smooth over this conflict. The harmonizer may settle emotional conflict by interjecting humor into the discussion, by remaining calm and placid in times of stress, and by smiling a lot.

It is the task of the harmonizer to smooth over conflict.

When ideas offered by the group members appear to be in conflict the harmonizer tries to show the compatibility of different points of view. He is the mediator of any disagreements that may occur. He is a peacemaker and compromiser.

The harmonizer brings a touch of stability to the group in times of stress and represents insurance for group cohesiveness and continued collaboration among the group members.

The Encourager. All human beings require a compliment now and then. A word of encouragement from someone in the discussion group always serves to reinforce and support individual effort, Many people hesitate to contribute to group discussion because they fear the disapproval of other group members.

The encourager functions to make people feel good about their participation in the problem solving team. He also helps ameliorate potential personality conflicts in the group, especially when a participant's suggestion is rejected by the group.

After someone has spoken and offered an idea for group consideration the encourager will say, "That was an extremely helpful idea, Jack. Thanks for your suggestion."

When the ideas of someone have been rejected by the group the encourager will try to find some aspect of the ideas to praise. "Although your ideas can't be pursued now, Mary," the encourager will say, "they do have quite a bit of merit and we ought to discuss them at some other time."

The Clarifier. One of the reasons why communication falters in groups is due to the fact that there is a difference between what is said and what is heard. In a group of eight people a speaker may say something and it is interpreted in seven different ways. This can lead to quite a bit of "beating about the bush" and not a little frustration.

The clarifier functions to minimize message distortion in a group. When someone says something that is particularly involved or complicated, the clarifier will repeat back the message to determine if the message has been properly received by group members. The clarifier might say, "Are you saying, Bob, (repeat the message here)" or "I heard you to say such and such, Phil, is that correct?"

After he has been questioned the member who has made an involved statement may wish to redesign his message for the benefit of the group members.

A group that is blessed with an active clarifier usually does not get bogged down in insignificant detail and in the task of sorting out misunderstandings.

A group that is blessed with an active clarifier usually does not get bogged down in insignificant detail and in the task of sorting out misunderstandings.

Gaining Skills for Group Discussion

How can members of a discussion group learn functional behaviors and how to avoid dysfunctional behaviors? Group members should be informed about both types of behavior and then asked to scrutinize their behavior patterns during group discussion. At times a simple awareness of functional and dysfunctional behaviors is sufficient to improve communication within the group.

Another way to focus attention on behaviors is to ask the evaluator to comment on functional and dysfunctional behaviors when he makes his post-session report. The evaluator, it must be cautioned, should not identify by name those members of the group who are behaving dysfunctionally.

To take the onus away from the evaluator, another strategem may be used: the behaviors evaluation sheet. The behaviors evaluation sheet is a brief instrument that can deliver feedback on behavior to each of the members of the group. Here is an example:

Behaviors Evaluation Sheet

Name of participant _____

Behavior	Yes	No	Behavior	Yes	No
Dominating	( )	( )	Building	( )	( )
Dropping out	( )	( )	Gate keeping	( )	( )
Blocking	( )	( )	Harmonizing	( )	( )
Distracting	( )	( )	Encouraging	( )	( )
			Clarifying	( )	( )

At the conclusion of every discussion session each of the members of the group should receive a blank behaviors evaluation sheet for every other member of the group. For example, if there are ten members in the discussion group, each member will receive nine behaviors evaluation sheets. The name of the participant who is evaluated appears at the heading of the sheet. The participant who is filling out the blank merely places check marks in appropriate places. It is not necessary to sign the sheet.

After the sheets have been filled out, someone collects the sheets and distributes them to the persons whose names appear at the head of the sheet. The feedback given to each person in the group should be private; it is not necessary for any group member to know how others in the group fared.

Conclusion

All of us pick up bad communications habits during our lives. Sometimes we are unaware of these bad habits. The only way bad habits can be corrected is first to become aware of them. In organizing a discussion group the good and bad habits of group members vis-a-vis group discussion should be pointed out. Good habits such as harmonizing, clarifying, gate keeping, and so forth, can then be emphasized; bad habits such as blocking, dominating, etc., can be corrected. When this happens the discussion session will become profitable in terms of time spent and satisfying to the adult learners.

13. Organizing Problem-Solving Groups

As we have seen, there are four major components to be taken into consideration when organizing discussion groups: 1) the organization of roles, 2) the organization of content, 3) the installation of norms, and 4) the organization of behaviors. These four components are necessary if the discussion group is to work effectively as a learning unit. The four components are also necessary for problem-solving groups. Instead of organizing the content or subject matter according to topic, goal, and outline, however, a different framework is suggested: a ten-step procedural model for group problem solving.

The strategy recommended in this chapter is simple: the group facilitator merely "unplugs" the topic-goal-outline component from the four-part system and "plugs in" the ten-step component for group problem solving.

Discussion System

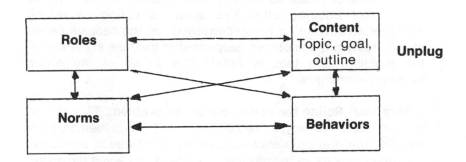

Problem-Solving System

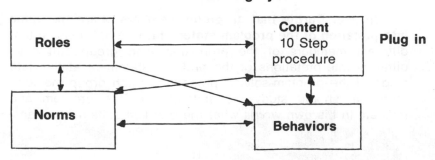

Lacking sufficient information about a problem situation, the problem-solving group is likely to jump to unwarranted conclusions.

Problem Solving: A Ten-Step Procedure

Step one: Gather information about the problem situation. Too often problem solving takes place in a knowledge vacuum; problem solvers frequently make no attempt to gather information and data about a situation that is problematic. Lacking sufficient information about a problem situation, the problem-solving group is likely to jump to unwarranted conclusions.

The information that is required for effective problem solving takes many forms. Perhaps the problem solvers should examine books and documents; perhaps they should investigate the ideas and feelings of others. There are many variables involved in every problem situation and these variables are usually interrelated. The problem-solving group must identify these variables and their interrelationships.

Step two: Formulate several statements of the problem. How a problem is formulated or expressed in a formal statement is of crucial importance. After information about the problem situation has been gathered, organized, and studied, the problem-solving group should state the problem in different ways. The formulation of several problem statements helps focus the attention of the group on different aspects of the problem situation.

Step three: Select the best statement of the problem. From an array of different formulations or statements of the problem the group should select the statement that best identifies the problem to be considered. The group decision should be made on the basis of group consensus. This means that there will be no conflict-reducing strategies such as voting or taking averages. In striving for group consensus on the best statement of the problem it sometimes happens that the new statement of the problem—one that is satisfactory to all of the group members—emerges.

Step four: Refine the statement of the problem. This step in the procedure may sometimes be left out. If group members are satisfied that the problem statement in step three is adequate, the group may move to step five; if there is still some misgiving about the manner in which the problem is formulated, it will be necessary to refine the statement of the problem.

Step five: Certify that all group members share the same interpretation of the problem statement. It is not unusual that different members of the problem-solving group still have different interpretations of the problem statement at this late stage of the problem-solving procedure. Each group member, therefore, should study the statement of the problem and indicate in his own words what the problem statement means.

The first five steps of the procedure largely concern the creation of a problem statement or formulation. The formulation is usually phrased in terms of a question that is to be answered by the group. Obviously a good deal of work is involved in formulating a problem question. Some may think that the amount of work is unjustified. I would point out again, however, that the formulation of the problem is of great importance. In counseling doctoral students regarding the preparation of their dissertations I have found that the hardest part of writing a dissertation is related to the statement of the problem. If the problem is stated accurately and with a degree of precision, the writing of the dissertation is relatively easy. If the statement of the problem is logically sloppy or inexact, the development of a dissertation is greatly hampered.

My experience with problem-solving groups is analogous to my experience with doctoral students. When groups are not very careful about formulating the statement of the problem, they usually invite all kinds of difficulties upon themselves.

Step six: Propose possible solutions to the problem. Once the problem has been stated in question form, the members of the problem-solving group should begin to list different responses to the question. Every question is amenable to different responses, depending on the perspectives of individuals in the group. These responses should be listed without unnecessary discussion or evaluation of each response.

Step seven: Anticipate the consequences of each possible solution. At the completion of step six the problem-solving group may have a list of several possible solutions or responses to the problem. The possible solutions should be listed on a chalkboard or butcher paper. Underneath each listed solution the problem-solving group should list the possible consequences that will derive from implementing the solution. For example, if three possible solutions are listed (A, B, and C), the group will "futurize" a bit and attempt to forecast consequences in terms of each of the solutions. "If A is implemented, this will result; if B is implemented, this will result; if C is implemented, this will result."

... if three possible solutions are listed (A, B, and C), the group will "futurize" a bit and attempt to forecast consequences in terms of each of the solutions.

Step eight: Select the best solution. Having weighed the relative merits of each possible solution in terms of probable outcomes, the problem solvers may now select a solution to be implemented. The group should also make plans for the implementation of the solution and assign implementation tasks to specific individuals. It should also be noted that the problem-solving group may select more than one solution for implementation.

Step nine: Implement the solution. Problem solving is purely academic and practically worthless unless it leads to action. After the decision-making process has been completed, appropriate action must be taken. The problem solvers should supervise the implementation of the course of action that has been selected as a response to the problem.

Step ten: Evaluate the outcomes. The best made plans of mice and men often go astray. Provision must be made by the problem-solving group to appraise the outcomes of the applied solution. If the solution works, the problem-solving activity may be terminated. If the solution does not work, the problem solvers must begin again at step one.

A Hypothetical Case

The ten-step procedure for organizing the content of group problem-solving activity is straightforward and simple enough, but a case study illustrating the procedure will elaborate and explain the procedure in more detail.

Let us suppose that at a particular church the adult education council is faced with a problem situation relating to low enrollments in the adult education program. The task of the council is to prescribe a remedy for low enrollments.

Step one: Gather information. Members of the adult education council decided to gather information about the problem situation. They attempted to locate indirect information by studying books and articles about adult education in the local church or parish. In so doing they gathered together a number of principles for program improvement and analyzed the views of others regarding declining enrollments. In effect they participated in the experiences of others who faced similar problem situations. Members of the council additionally met with prospective learners and asked questions about their participation or lack of participation in the adult education program. This strategy provided some direct information about the problem situation.

Step two: Formulation. The members of the adult education council met after they had attempted to gain background information about the problem situation. Four problem statements were formulated by the members of the council:

1. What is wrong with our adult education program?
2. Why is participation in our adult education program so limited?
3. How can we acquire better textbooks for our adult education program?
4. How can adult education programs be improved?

Let us suppose that at a particular church the adult education council is faced with a problem situation relating to low enrollments in the adult education program. The task of the council is to prescribe a remedy for low enrollments.

Step three: Selection of problem statement. The adult education council next determined to select the problem statement that best expressed the problem situation. In order to do this they submitted each of the problem statements to a careful analysis. It was decided that the first problem statement assumed too much. Perhaps nothing was wrong with the program as such. There could be a number of reasons why participation in the program was low and these reasons could have little to do with the program itself, e.g., lack of knowledge about the program on the part of prospective learners.

The second problem statement was not a bad question to ask when gathering background information, but the statement was not action-oriented. Suppose the council members discovered "why" participation was marginal. Their task would be complete when they arrived at a speculative response to the question. It was also thought that the question was much too general and unfocused.

The third question assumed that the lack of good textbooks was the cause or condition of poor participation in the program. Again, such questions as these are almost useless for problem solving.

The fourth question appeared to be the best statement of the problem. Some of the members of the council were not enthusiastic about the manner in which the question was formulated, but they agreed to move on to the next step in the problem-solving procedure.

Step four: Refinement of the statement. Some of the members of the council, at the time they were gathering background information, discovered in their reading that plans for the promotion of adult education programs must be well laid and executed. Good programs without good promotion do not attract large numbers of participants. Other members of the council learned, when they were discussing the program with potential participants, that some adults did not know about the program while other adults thought the adult education program was mainly for the "in" group, the church pillars.

After discussing the problem statement further, the members of the council decided to refine the statement to read: "How can we attract more participants for our adult education program?" The original statement of the problem—"How can adult education programs be improved?"—was changed from a consideration of adult education programs in general to a consideration of **our** adult education program. The concept of program improvement was interpreted in the sense of improving program promotion and publicity. The refined statement of the problem was also more action-oriented.

Step five: Interpretation. Each of the members of the council was asked to repeat back the statement of the problem in his or her own words to assure that all of the members of the council interpreted the statement in the same manner. After a brief discussion it was decided that all of the council members shared the same interpretation of the statement. (The problem statement offered in this example is not very complex and it may be wondered how it could be misinterpreted. Sometimes, however, members of problem-solving groups do not always see or hear the actual problem statement; they entertain in their "heads" a problem statement that is quite different from the actual one. In the present example, one of the members of the council was asked to repeat the problem statement in his own words and he said, "We are asking a question about how we can make our program more attractive." This is greatly different from the actual statement; the actual statement concerns attracting **people** to the program and not **curriculum** attractiveness.)

Step six: Possible solutions. Addressing themselves to the problem statement the members of the council generated the following possible solutions:

1. Ask the pastor to remind people of the program on Sundays.
2. Send letters to all potential participants.
3. Since people think they get nothing when they pay nothing, charge a small tuitional fee.
4. Perform a needs/interests assessment and base the next program on the identified needs and interests of potential participants.
5. Make posters advertising the program and display the posters in church.
6. Organize a telephone committee to invite potential participants personally.
7. Organize the geographical area served by the church into neighborhood units; ask neighborhood captains to extend personal invitations to the potential participants.

Step seven: Forecasting. The members of the council examined each of the possible solutions in terms of the consequences likely to develop out of the implementation of the solutions. The following chart was drawn to display both the possible solutions and consequences.

| 1. Pulpit announcement. | 1. Only those present in church would hear the announcement. Announcement may get lost among other announcements. |

2. Letters.	2. Written invitation would make a good impression; people would have a notice at home for reference when scheduling social activities, meetings, etc.
3. Fee.	3. People would be likely to think that the major purpose of the program was money-making.
4. Needs interests assessment.	4. Assessment would stimulate possible enthusiasm for program; program would become more relevant to potential participants.
5. Posters.	5. Would be seen only by those in church; would probably lack impact.
6. Telephone committee.	6. Some people would be disturbed; commercial enterprises overuse the telephone; possible negative effect; too impersonal.
7. Neighborhood units.	7. Direct, personal contact would be impactful; personal invitations from neighbor would be effective in promoting good will.

The members of the council discussed the chart in some detail. Eventually the council was ready to move on to step eight.

Step eight: Selection of solution. The adult education council decided that they could attract more participants to the program in two ways: 1) by basing future programs more on the needs and interests of the participants and 2) by organizing neighborhood units for promotional purposes. A division of labor plan was worked out and specific members of the council were assigned particular tasks.

Step nine: Implementation. The plan for problem solution was carried out.

Step ten: Evaluation. Since the problem was remediated—participation in the next program grew by 83%—it was judged that the solution was correct.

Conclusion

The example which illustrated the ten-step procedure for problem-solving groups was sketchy, but adequate to convey the substance of the procedure. Group problem solving is sometimes very taxing, very difficult, and extremely complicated; an individual is more likely to reach a solution to a problem sooner than a group. In a group, however, there is a greater amount of information available and a greater number of different approaches to the problem situation. Group problem solving increases acceptance of and commitment to the problem solution. Group problem solving holds an important place in adult education. The framework presented in this chapter will hopefully facilitate the endeavors of problem-solving groups.

14. Teacher Decisions: A Matter of Style

The teacher of adults is called upon to perform many functions. One of the primary functions of the teacher is decision making. In this chapter I shall discuss teacher decision making in adult education in the context of different decision-making styles. Various styles will be identified, styles appropriate for different educational settings will be noted, and suggestions will be offered regarding the most appropriate decision-making style for adult religious education.

Five Basic Styles

A review of research and literature on the concept of leadership assisted me in delineating five basic decision-making styles of the teacher of adults: 1) dominative, 2) persuasive, 3) consultative, 4) consensual, and 5) conformative.

The Dominative Style. The dominative teacher is autocratic. He makes all decisions relating to the course of study and informs the learners of these decisions. To say that he is autocratic does not necessarily mean that he is not congenial. One does not need to manifest the behavior of a bear to qualify for the tag of autocrat. The dominative teacher is concerned principally with communicating his decisions to the learners and is not overly concerned with gathering learner support for his decisions. His decisions are usually transmitted to students by means of mandate or instructional fiat.

The Persuasive Style. The persuasive teacher makes all decisions affecting the course of study, communicates these decisions to the learners, and attempts to persuade them that these decisions are best. The decisions of the persuasive teacher will not be changed because of learner input, but the persuasive teacher wants to involve the learners at least to the extent of persuading them to ratify or affirm his decisions.

The Consultative Style. Prior to making a decision regarding the implementation of a course of study the consultative teacher calls the learners together and asks them for input. Learner input is treated as advice that may be accepted or rejected. In the last analysis it is the teacher who makes decisions about the course after he has gathered information and opinions from the learners. The consultative teacher elicits ideas from the learners

A review of research and literature on the concept of leadership assisted me in delineating five basic decision-making styles of the teacher of adults: 1) dominative, 2) persuasive, 3) consultative, 4) consensual, and 5) conformative.

and takes these ideas into account before he actualizes decisions.

The Consensual Style. The consensual teacher becomes a member of the class and enters into dialogue with the learners. The learning group, including the teacher, arrives at decisions based on group consensus. The teacher enjoys input into the decision-making process only as a member of the group. He may veto a decision not because he is the teacher but because everyone in the group has veto power.

The Conformative Style. Operating out of a conformative style the teacher permits/encourages the learners to make decisions about the management of the course of study. The teacher simply conforms to the decisions made by the learners and legitimizes these decisions. The teacher decides to do what the learners want him to do relating to the development of the course. The teacher apprises himself mainly as an organizer and facilitator of group decision making. His instructional decisions are directly contingent upon the decisions of the learners.

Decision Styles: A Continuum

A teacher of adults may vary from one style to another in decision making. Usually, however, a prevailing or dominant decision style will emerge. The prevailing decision style of teachers of adults may be charted on a continuum in order to understand the implications of each of the five basic styles.

Let **A**-dominative, **B**-persuasive, **C**-consultative, **D**-consensual, and **E**-conformative. Also, let **x** equal the "conservative" end of the continuum and **y** equal the "liberal" end of the continuum.

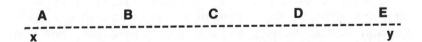

Toward the **x** end of the continuum the teacher possesses much control; the learners are allowed little or no freedom; the learners are asked for little or no input into the decision-making process; the teacher is active while the learners are passive vis-a-vis decision-making; little time is consumed in the decision-making process; participation of the learners in the decision-making process is nonexistent or marginal.

Toward the **y** end of the continuum the teacher possesses little control; the learners are permitted a greater degree of freedom; the learners are able to provide much input into the decision-making process; the learners are active while the teacher may be only marginally active; the decision-making process consumes much time; participation of the learners is high.

Twenty-Five Styles

The matter of teacher decision style would be complex enough if only five styles were involved. It must be remembered, however, that I indicated there were five **basic** styles. There are, in fact, 25 different styles that must be taken into consideration.

Within the framework of a course of study two kinds of decisions must be made: 1) decisions about specific goals, desired outcomes, or products, and 2) decisions about goal paths, methods to reach goals, and processes which conduce to the realization of products. In essence decisions must be made about the "message" of the course and the "medium" employed to convey the message. A teacher, for example, may be dominative regarding course goals and consensual regarding methods to reach these goals; he may be persuasive regarding course goals and conformative regarding the processes which produce these goals.

The following chart displays decision-making styles. Again, let **A**-dominative, **B**-persuasive, **C**-consultative, **D**-consensual, and **E**-conformative.

There are, in fact, 25 different styles that must be taken into consideration.

Goal Path Decisions (Process)

Goal Decisions (Product)	Dominative	Persuasive	Consultative	Consensual	Conformative
Dominative	A/A	A/B	A/C	A/D	A/E
Persuasive	B/A	B/B	B/C	B/D	B/E
Consultative	C/A	C/B	C/C	C/D	C/E
Consensual	D/A	D/B	D/C	D/D	D/E
Conformative	E/A	E/B	E/C	E/D	E/E

The style **A/A** teacher is dominative both in deciding goals and goal paths; a style **A/B** teacher is dominative in deciding goals and persuasive in regard to goal paths or methods; a style **A/C** teacher is dominative in deciding goals and consultative in regard to goal paths; a style **A/D** teacher is dominative in deciding goals and consensual in regard to goal paths; a style **A/E** teacher is dominative in deciding goals and conformative in regard to goal paths. Each of the cells in the typological chart may be explained in a similar manner.

Which Style is Most Effective?

Given the proclivity in adult education to promote learner participation in a way usually not characteristic of childhood education, and given a tendency to prefer democratic over autocratic leadership styles, we are tempted to discount dominative and persuasive decision styles in favor of styles at the other end of the continuum. But a simple answer cannot be offered to the inquiry about most effective style. Consideration of a host of variables must enter into the judgment about most effective style.

We must consider, first of all, the context in which the teaching-learning is to take place: time constraints, nature of the course offering, size of the class, nature of the educational system, and so forth. We must also consider the learners: temperament of the learners, status of their morale, competencies of the learners, information possessed by the learners, etc.

We must consider, first of all, the context in which the teaching-learning is to take place; time constraints, nature of the course offering, size of the class, nature of the educational system, and so forth. We must also consider the learners; temperment of the learners, status of their morale, conpetencies of the learners, information possessed by the learners, etc.

Is there sufficient time, given the time constraints imposed by scheduling, to initiate consultative, consensual, or conformative styles? What is the class size? The teacher may operate in one mode of decision making in a class of 50 learners and in another style in a class of five learners. What kind of style is expected of the teacher by the educational system (a university, for example) or by a subsystem (a department within the university)?

Will the same style be effective in different educational settings: in training classes in industry, orientation or inservice courses in hospitals, discussion clubs in local churches, graduate courses in a school of medicine? Will it not be necessary to adapt decisions style to meet the exigencies of different concrete situations?

What are the feelings of the learners regarding participatory decision making? Are the learners competent enough to participate productively in decision making? Will the moral of the learners be affected adversely if they are not permitted, in some way, to participate in the decision making that creates the teaching-learning environment? Do the learners possess adequate information for decision making? Are they equipped with skills for group decision making?

These and similar questions must be answered before a teacher consciously plans to adopt a specific decision-making style. In other words, the situation must be carefully diagnosed before a specific mode of decision making is prescribed.

Some Examples

Although it is extremely difficult to prescribe specific decision styles in general terms, some examples of appropriate decision styles may be delineated.

Example 1: A teacher of adults in industry has been given the task by his superiors to instruct a group of forty assembly-line workers on a highly technical matter. He must complete the instruction under severe institutional restraints; he has been allowed two hours to complete the instruction. The learners have never before been involved in decision making regarding technical instruction courses and they do not expect to be so involved.

In a situation such as this the instructor has no choice but to tend toward the dominative style in both selecting instructional goals and goal paths. He simply does not have time to persuade the learners that his decisions are correct; **a fortiori** he does not have time to consult with them. Instructional goals have already been set by the system, thereby precluding the possibility of meeting with the learners to form a group consensus.

Example 2: An assistant superintendent of schools has been assigned the task of training teachers on the use of a new instructional technique. Instructional goals have been set by the school system in the person of the superintendent. The assistant superintendent is told that he may determine how much time is needed for a workshop to train 20 teachers.

The teacher (assistant superintendent) must be dominative or persuasive in deciding instructional goals; he is more or less constrained to decide to affirm the goals set by the system. On the other hand, he has plenty of time to meet with the twenty teachers on a consultative, consensual, or conformative basis to determine how the goals will be met. The learners are all experienced teachers and should have some good ideas on how to reach the instructional goals that have been assigned.

Example 3: A university professor is teaching an advanced graduate seminar in 19th-century American history. The professor wishes to provide a variety of seminar presentations through the use of various educational techniques. He assigns specific techniques to individuals in the seminar, but permits them to select topics within the area of study. In effect he has exercised dominative decision style in regard to goal paths and conformative decision style in regard to goals.

Example 4: A pastor has been asked to moderate a group discussion club. Since the members of the club attend on a strictly voluntary basis, he decides to encourage them to select their own educational goals. Since the members of the group are creative and knowledgeable persons, the pastor also decides to encourage them to determine **how** they want to reach the goals. In this example the pastor will operate out of a conformative style both in regard to goals and goal paths.

The examples given above illustrate how different decision styles can be adopted for different educational settings and with different kinds of learners. Given the fact that there is an almost infinite number of possible educational settings and an equally indefinite number of possible groups of learners, the prevailing decision style that **should** be adopted can be selected only after examining the educational situation. And by educational situation is meant the complexus of factors that constitute the total environment of the teaching-learning situation.

Decision Style and Religious Education

While each educational situation is different from the next, general categories of educational situations can be identified. One of these categories is adult religious education. Adult education that takes place in the setting of the parish or local church is obviously different from adult education that takes place in industry, in hospitals, in universities, in prisons, and in technical schools.

The kind of adult education that occurs in the setting of the local church or parish is differentiated from other kinds of adult education by reason of the typical subject matter studied by the learners. But the characteristic that looms largest in distinguishing adult religious education from many other kinds of adult education is the fact that adult religious education is **voluntary.** Learners are not rewarded by remuneration or promise of job improvement or the acquisition of a technical skill when they take part in adult education in the religious setting. People participate in church-sponsored adult education because they wish to satisfy some needs not associated with the economic necessity of making a living. This factor, above all others, must be kept in mind by teachers of adults when they determine decision-making style.

Furthermore, people will tolerate dominative instructional styles when they are not free to do otherwise, e.g., trainees in a job setting. But people will not usually abide with dominative styles when they have the opportunity of not participating in a course. (This is not to justify necessarily the use of dominative styles in certain situations but merely to point out a fact of life.)

The first general principle for the teacher of adults in the church setting, then, is this: **Do not exercise dominative styles either in goal setting or the selection of goal paths.**

The second principle is similar to the first: **Permit adult learners to be as self-directing as possible by inviting them to participate as fully as possible in the decision-making process.**

This implies that the teacher of adults will at least exercise consultative styles and will hopefully function according to consensual or conformative styles.

People participate in church-sponsored adult education because they wish to satisfy some needs not associated with the economic necessity of making a living. This factor, above all others, must be kept in mind, by teachers of adults when they determine decision-making style.

Note well that the principle states adult learners should be permitted to be as self-directing **as possible.** In some contexts, even in the church setting or voluntary situation, the teacher of adults will not be able to exercise anything but the consultative style. For example, if 80 people show up for a five session course of study on the New Testament, the teacher will not have sufficient time to form a consensus or to determine **as a group** what they want to learn about the New Testament and how they will learn it.

Again, a context that could call for the exercise of persuasive decision style can easily be imagined. Suppose a pastor has identified some institutional need of the participants in a program, a need that the participants cannot see because their perspectives are too narrow. The teacher will set goals and attempt to persuade the participants that the attainment of these goals will help them become more productive members of the parish or local church.

Finally, suppose again that a teacher of adults is dealing with adult learners who have no conception of educational goal paths besides that of the lecture technique. The teacher may wish to persuade the learners that they should employ the discussion technique or other techniques, as goal paths for reaching instructional goals.

What I am saying is essentially this: Adult learners should be encouraged to control courses of study through participative decision making within the parameters established by the total situation. One of the greatest outcomes of adult education of any kind is the growth of freedom in the learners. This cannot be accomplished when learners are consistently "unfree" in the teaching-learning situation.

Conclusion

What is important about the discussion of teacher decision styles presented in this chapter is that there are other decision styles besides the dominative style, something that all teachers of adults should remember. "We teach as we were taught," is an adage that is unfortunately true in many instances. Since during childhood education many future teachers of adults were exposed to only one style of teacher decision making—the dominative style—a goodly number of these teachers of adults conduct themselves as pedagogues and not as andragogues. They manage the teaching-learning situation according to monarchical rather than democratic principles. If the teaching of adults in church settings is to improve, learners must be brought into the decision-making processes that create the learning climate whenever this is possible and feasible. And the reason for this suggestion is that learner involvement in decision making facilitates in the learners a sense of their own dignity and freedom—one of the most important outcomes of adult education.

Note well that the principle states adult learners should be permitted to be as self-directing *as possible.*

Since during childhood education many future teachers of adults were exposed to only one style of teacher decision making—the dominative style—a goodly number of these teachers of adults conduct themselves as pedagogues and not as andragogues.

15. A Climate for Adult Learning

If learning means anything it means change: change in cognitive structure or knowledge, change in attitude, and/or change in behavior. Learning means change that is observable and change that is unobservable, change that is manifested in different learner behavior and change within the learner that cannot be directly assessed. Learning means immediate change and change that may not be recognized for many years after the learning experience.

I part company, and gladly so, with those educational empiricists who define learning strictly in terms of observable changes that occur as immediate outcomes of the learning experience. They have lusted after the approaches of the "hard" sciences and have, I believe, fallen prey to a type of reductionism that is concerned only with externals, a reductionism that ignores human interiority and introspection. But this is not precisely the place to enter into a philosophical joust with those who define learning in a preposterously narrow sense. Suffice it to say that learning is not amenable to easy definition.

Learning means change. It is one of the principal tasks of the teacher of adults, therefore, to facilitate change. And one of the ways of facilitating change is to construct a milieu, an environment, or a climate for change. It will be the burden of this chapter to outline some characteristics of a climate for adult learning, a climate that is particularly suitable for adult education in the setting of the local church or parish.

The word climate usually refers to meteorological conditions, at least the first two dictionary definitions of climate refer to the environment produced by the weather. In this chapter I use the word climate in a broader, psychological sense. The conditions described as normative for producing an adequate climate for adult learning will be largely psychological in nature.

Most of the conditions recommended in this chapter have been suggested, in different words, by other writers. I am indebted to Gerald Pine and Peter Horne's article "Principles and Conditions for Learning in Adult Education,"[1] to Malcolm

I part company, and gladly so, with those educational empiricists who define learning strictly in terms of observable changes that occur as immediate outcomes of the learning experience.

[1] Pine, Gerald and Horne, Peter, "Principles and Conditions for Learning in Adult Education," Adult Leadership, Vol. 18, No. 4, 1969, pp. 108-110.

Knowles' *The Adult Learner: A Neglected Species,*[2] to Harry Miller's *Teaching and Learning in Adult Education,*[3] and to J.R. Kidd's *How Adults Learn.*[4] Those who are particularly interested in the nature of adult learning would do well to assimilate the ideas contained in these resources. Most of all, though, I am indebted to my own experience as a teacher of adults. My list of conditions for the facilitation of learning, I note, is not merely a report of what others have written.

Condition 1: Relevancy

Adult learners should feel a sense of the relevancy of the educational activities and goals.

Nothing impedes learning by adults more than a feeling, sometimes unarticulated, that **what** they are going to gain from a program is irrelevant to their lives. This, of course, is another way of saying that educational objectives must be firmly based on the needs and interests of the learners. Programs that serve only institutional needs and interests, without reference to the individual learners' consciousness of their needs and interests, will ordinarily be perceived as irrelevant. Adult learners must be brought to a consciousness of institutional needs and interests as coincidental with their self-perceived needs and interests before the will to learn becomes operative. I mention the relevancy of educational goals in terms of individual needs and interests and institutional needs and interests because I strongly suspect that many programs in the context of the local churches or parishes are oriented more toward the satisfaction of institutional needs. It would be naive of all of us to entertain the idea that "adult religious education" has not sometimes been the descriptor for what is in fact indoctrination and propaganda.

The activities and tasks which help learners achieve goals must also be relevant and meaningful to the adult learners. Means in adult education are just as important as ends; the process is just as important as the product. The goals of an educational activity can be highly meaningful to the learners, but when the activity itself—the technique employed by the teacher—is perceived as lacking relevance to the needs and

Adult learners must be brought to a consciousness of institutional needs and interests as coincidental with their self-perceived needs and interests before the will to learn becomes operative.

[2]Knowles, Malcolm, *The Adult Learner: A Neglected Species,* Houston: Gulf Publishing Co., 1973.

[3]Miller, Harry, *Teaching and Learning in Adult Education,* New York: Macmillan, 1971 (7th printing).

[4]Kidd, J.R., *How Adults Learn,* New York: Association Press, 1973.

interests of the learners, the entire educational enterprise stands in danger of collapse.

An example of irrelevancy regarding process or means is easy to frame. The lecture technique has been vastly overused in adult education. This is true of adult religious education, adult education in industry, adult education in the university context, and so forth. Many adult learners have needs for social interaction in the learning situation; they have needs for active participation in the learning process. Very often these needs are not met by teachers who constantly lecture.

Condition 2: Comfort

Adult learners should feel physically comfortable. Over the years I have collected evaluative feedback from adult learners during courses and workshops and at the conclusion of courses and workshops. Adult learners have been quick to point out that they were physically uncomfortable in many cases. Physical discomfort experienced by the learners is often responsible for psychological discomfort. A person who is distressed by a cold room, inadequate lighting, cramped seating in an undersized desk, and noise from a room next door soon becomes psychologically "turned off."

The "little things" that promote the comfort of the adult learners are very important. The "little things" that cause physical discomfort and associated psychological reactions can effectively destroy climates for learning that are otherwise perfect. To quote Dr. Paul Bergevin, "in adult education trivial things are never trivial."

Condition 3: Interactions

The interactions between teacher and learners, and among learners, should be characterized by mutual trust, acceptance, and respect.

Good human relationships are crucial to any human undertaking. The relationship between teacher and learners must be friendly, warm, and open. Since the best resources for education are human resources, the relationships among the learners should promote teamwork and collaboration.

Three concepts are basic to the kind of relationships I have in mind: trust, acceptance, and respect. When I trust someone, it means that I let down my guard and be myself. I neither hide behind formality nor office. At its highest levels trust means that I am willing to become vulnerable in regard to those who are trusted. When I am trustful it means I present myself genuinely to others without recourse to playacting or subterfuge.

Acceptance means that teacher and learners are willing to receive one another as unique individuals regardless of differing opinions or conflicting ideas. In the teaching-learning situation serious disagreements may emerge, but these disagreements become defused and limited from causing serious interpersonal difficulties because personal acceptance is the operative norm.

Respect means that teacher and learners value the insights and ideas of one another, that deference is paid to everyone in the teaching-learning situation because: 1) everyone possesses human dignity, 2) all adults are relatively experienced and judgmentally mature, and 3) collaborative learning can be accomplished only where mutual courtesy obtains.

Condition 4: Active Participation

Adult learners should participate actively in the learning process.

Research has suggested that informational data can be transmitted just as effectively through the lecture technique as the group discussion technique. Two questions must be raised in the light of such research: 1) Is learning to be equated with the transmission of information? 2) Is passive learning more **worthwhile** than active learning? I advise that both of these questions should be answered in the negative.

The learning process is more than merely passing on information from teacher to learner. Learners, especially adult learners, can acquire a subtle kind of knowledge simply through interacting with one another. Effective learning can take place more readily when people communicate together, work together, and solve problems together. There is a principle in group dynamics that applies here. If you want to change anyone's behavior, get that person to give loyalty to a group; human interchange in the group will do the rest. Educators must be concerned, as Alfred North Whitehead pointed out, not only with abstractions but also with feelings; not only with headwork, but heartwork as well. While **some** kinds of technical training can be accomplished effectively through the "teacher-tell-me" technique, the kind of education that usually takes place in the church setting requires more than learners who merely listen to what a lecturer has to say.

Activity in learning is more valuable than passivity. One of the major side-effects of adult learning should be the transformation of the acquiescent adult into the assertive adult. Acquiescence and tight-lipped timidity is not characteristic of the mature person. Any form of education that insists on the passivity of the learners promotes in the learners a self-concept that is not in accordance with the best principles of adult education.

What I am saying here is simply this: the process of adult learning is, in many ways, the product of adult learning. If the process of adult learning is such that it encourages passivity, inaction, and submission, the learners will learn how to be

If you want to change anyone's behavior, get that person to give loyalty to a group; human interchange in the group will do the rest.

passive, inactive, and submissive—despite what they may learn about the so-called content of the learning process.

Condition 5: Positive Feedback

Adult learners should receive positive feedback from one another and from the teacher.

The term feedback is relatively new in common usage and is related to the functioning of machine or computer systems. As the word is used here it simply means "evaluative reaction." Feedback can be of two kinds: positive (praising, encouraging) or negative (correcting, adjusting).

We may be inclined to think that since the learners are adults, there is no need for the teacher or other learners to take time to offer positive feedback as a reaction to adequate performance. Again, we may be tempted to think that adults are fairly well self-confident and have no need for anyone to say "Well done!" when they do a good job. Just the opposite is true. A commentator on the psychology of Alfred Adler once summed up Adler's psychology by saying, "Behind the face of every general or diplomat there is a small child." No matter how old or how mature we may be, we are still social animals and need positive feedback. In the most mature of persons, a remnant of self-doubt remains. (Perhaps this is not necessarily all bad!)

When adult learners manifest behavior that is desirable or even adequate, they should be given positive reinforcement and encouragement. The slightest accomplishments and achievements of adult learners should not be passed over silently. Encouragement of the learner, I think, is the stuff out of which evolves learner progress.

A commentator on the psychology of Alfred Adler once summed up Adler's psychology by saying, "Behind the face of every general or diplomat there is a small child." No matter how old or how mature we may be, we are still social animals and need positive feedback.

Condition 6: Negative Feedback

Adult learners should be offered negative feedback in such a way that the feedback does not bruise their feelings.

It happens sometimes that adult learners must be corrected. When they do something that does not meet the minimum performance standards or when they espouse a point of view that is thoroughly discredited, e.g., the earth is flat, they should be told so. A teacher of adults can win many accolades for being a "nice guy" if he never offers negative feedback for the learners to ponder; he can also be responsible for much learner stultification. At times we can grow and change only in the wake of negative feedback.

Criticism and negative feedback, however, must be couched in tactful terms. The teacher of adults should be careful (carefull) when he offers negative feedback. The purpose of negative feedback is not to injure, deflate egos, or produce hurt feelings; negative feedback is provided for the sake of learner improvement.

At times we can grow and change only in the wake of negative feedback.

It would seem to some that adults have gone beyond the stage where criticism and negative feedback have the potential for hurting feelings. Such is not the case universally. Some adults may be able to abide comfortably with negative feedback; others have a hard time living with criticism. Some people are thick-skinned; others are very sensitive to criticism and must be handled gently.

In essence the rule advised here is the simple rule of kindness and gentleness when offering negative feedback.

Condition 7: Freedom

Adult learners must feel a sense of freedom in the learning situation.

In the memories of many people "school days" are reminiscent of days of regimentation and strict control. They sat at their desks, fidgeted and fussed under the threat of reprisal, and raised their hands every time they wanted to shed the moral leash that constrained them. "School days" were days of unfreedom.

The atmosphere of freedom must permeate the adult teaching-learning situation, particularly when the learners have volunteered for participation in a program. Learners should be free to speak out, to move to more comfortable chairs, to challenge ideas, to assist in setting goals for learning, to volunteer information without raising their hands; learners should be free to do a thousand things that would be unthinkable in the so-called traditional elementary classroom.

It makes little difference what the manifest content of the course may be; the latent content of every adult learning enterprise should be freedom.

Learner freedom in the learning process is important because one of the overarching goals of adult education is the increased freedom of the learners. This goal of freedom or liberation is seldom articulated in the course prospectus, but it is there nonetheless. It makes little difference what the manifest content of the course may be; the latent content of every adult learning enterprise should be freedom.

Now people do not become free and more liberated when they are involved in a context that imposes restrictions and constraints upon their freedom. If people are to become free, they must be permitted to exercise freedom. If people are to become mature, they must be treated as mature persons. One way not to teach freedom is to restrain, restrict, and regiment the learners; one way not to teach maturity is to apprise the learners as immature.

Condition 8: Self-Dependence

Adult learners should feel a sense of self-dependence.

One of the primary counterproductive features of the traditional schooling many of us experienced as children was our sense of dependency on the teacher. In a very real sense our lack of self-dependency and lack of freedom were mutually supportive. We looked to the teacher for questions, since we were reluctant to ask our own, and for the answers to the questions the teacher posed. We were not encouraged to rely on our life-experience for solutions to problems, probably because we had so dearly little life-experience. We depended more on what teacher said and on the printed word than on individual discovery and personal reflection.

While adults are generally self-dependent and self-directing in many areas of life, they can very easily be led into a childish dependence on the teacher. This is attributable, I suppose, to the fact that as children they were trained so well in dependency. Adult education at its worst can be "school days" revisited; many adults can be made to entertain an unreasonable dependency on the teacher. Since self-dependence is a sign of maturity, the adult learning situations should be so organized as to provide adults the opportunities of becoming more mature through self-dependency, a sense of enterprise, resourcefulness, and creativity. Adult education should not be solely what "teacher says." It should afford the learners the wherewithal to ask questions, to search, to discover, and to practice self-reliance. In such a milieu authentic adult education takes place.

Condition 9: Collaboration

Adult learners should collaborate in attaining educational goals.

Competition is as American as apple pie. We are taught to compete for grades in school, for trophies on the athletic fields, and for jobs in the workaday world. If there is any spirit that is pervasive in American life it is the spirit of competition. Such a spirit is not necessarily all bad, but it can get out of hand.

The climate for adult learning should foster collaboration and serve to regulate or minimize the spirit of competition. Adult learners should be "helping" kinds of people, ready and willing to assist their co-learners at all times. Many hands make light work and many minds working together on the same problem produce good outcomes. Once I noticed a sign hanging in a professor's office. The sign heralded this message: All of us together are smarter than each of us alone. This bit of wisdom could almost serve as a motto for adult learners.

The climate for adult learning should foster collaboration and serve to regulate or minimize the spirit of competition.

Condition 10: Tolerance for Ambiguity

Adult learners should tolerate ambiguity in the learning situation.

Many adults view education in terms of intellectual recipes to be assimilated, easy answers to be memorized, and absolute statements to be learned. This is especially true of adults who were exposed as children to the type of schooling that fostered a fear of ambiguity, unanswered questions, and unsolved problems.

When both teacher and adult learners have a healthy respect for the complexity of life, ambiguity will be tolerated and the myriad aspects of every question will be examined intelligently. What everyone in the teaching-learning situation must recognize is this: we see now in a glass darkly. Clearcut answers to many of life's problems are not easily obtained; we must live with obscurity.

The issue is raised here because some persons think that success in education is measured by the number of answers the learners discover. Quite often educational success is measured by the number and quality of questions that are brought forth, investigated, and discussed.

Quite often educational success is measured by the number and quality of questions that are brought forth, investigated, and discussed.

Conclusion

The conditions identified above are phrased as normative or "should" statements regarding the adult learner. The climate for learning should support and emphasize these normative statements. An ideal climate for learning will foster in the learners a sense of relevancy, physical comfort, trustful relationships, active participation of the learners, positive feedback, careful negative feedback, freedom of inquiry, a sense of self-dependence, collaboration, and will support a tolerance for ambiguity. The ideal climate for learning may never be attained, but the ideal climate must always be the goal of the teacher and learners in adult education.

16. Some Techniques for Adult Education

In chapter six the distinction was made between method and technique. A method, it will be recalled, is a way of organizing learners administratively. Verner[1] identified correspondence study, directed individual study, apprenticeship, and internship as individual methods. Small group methods are the class, the discussion group, and the laboratory or group experiential learning situation. Large group methods include the assembly or workshop and the convention.

I suggested also in chapter six that techniques were ways of organizing people for learning and that techniques are employed within the framework of a given method. I indicated further that techniques could be subsumed under two headings: instrumental and non-instrumental techniques. The difference between the two kinds of techniques lies in the use or non-use of "things" for organizing people for learning. When a teacher shows a film to a group of adult learners, he is employing an instrument for the patterning of communications. When a teacher asks adult learners to roleplay a specific situation, he is simply organizing the learners according to a definite structure or plan.

In the present chapter I shall list and comment on various instrumental and non-instrumental techniques. This will be followed by some general guidelines for the selection of techniques.

Instrumental Techniques

Techniques for teaching and learning in adult education are instrumental when a device or mechanism is employed. These devices or mechanisms are usually known as electronic media. The following remarks about instrumental techniques, at any rate, will be restricted to electronic media. Films, filmstrips, overhead projections, opaque projections, and audio tapes (the media I have chosen for commentary in this chapter) are typically employed: 1) to present information or factual data, 2) to stimulate interest in a subject matter, and/or 3) to elicit responses from the learners. These approaches are used alone

[1] Verner, Coolie, *A Conceptual Scheme for the Identification and Classification of Processes,* Chicago: Adult Education Association of the U.S.A., 1962, pp. 9f.

134

usually within the framework of individual methods; when instrumental techniques are employed with groups of learners, they are almost always used in combination with other techniques, e.g., group discussion following the showing of a film.

Film. Films have been used for adult education for many years and there seems to be no sign that this approach to education is suffering a loss in popularity. An effective film can do much to convey information to viewers, stimulate enthusiasm for a topic, and to encourage learners to respond in group discussions following the showing of the film. Since we are living increasingly in an era of the image, films can be put to good use in adult education.

The problem with using films as a technique for teaching-learning is that they are usually too expensive to purchase. This means that films must be reserved in advance of showing, rented, and usually mailed to the educator. Films must be rewound and mailed back to the distributor. In my 17 years as a teacher I have been disappointed more than several times when the film I wanted was not available, or when postal service failed to deliver a film in time for a class.

When films are used with adult learners, the films should be short (15-30 minutes) and should be yoked with another technique that involves learners more actively in the learning process.

Filmstrip. A filmstrip is a series of small individual frames arranged in a permanent sequence on a strip of 35mm film. The audio portion of a filmstrip program is usually transcribed on a record or audio tape. Filmstrips are almost always purchased. They are easily shown and handled, and storage is no problem. An individual filmstrip usually runs 15-25 minutes.

I have always favored the use of filmstrips largely because of the availability of multitudes of excellent productions. The filmstrip projection is not as dramatic as a film projection since there are no "moving" pictures. But filmstrip projections can be visual treats if they are prepared with a thought to artistry.

Filmstrip packages sometimes contain as many as six or eight individual filmstrips. Each of the individual filmstrips focuses on a sub-topic of the theme considered in the filmstrip package. It would be a mistake, I suggest, to show all of the individual filmstrips of a package together. As with the film, the filmstrip should be employed in conjunction with other techniques.

Overhead Projector. The overhead projector came into general use in the 1930's as a device to display publicly the scores of bowlers. If you have ever been in a bowling alley during a tournament, you will know immediately what an overhead projector is. In many ways the overhead projector may

When films are used with adult learners, the films should be short (15-30 minutes) and should be yoked with another technique that involves learners more actively in the learning process.

be substituted for the chalkboard. The teacher stands in front of the room under normal lighting conditions and displays 10 x 10 transparencies that have been prepared beforehand. Using a grease pencil the teacher may write on the transparencies; this writing will be projected onto the screen.

Overhead projections are useful for displaying charts, figures, and outlines during a lecture. Many teachers, in fact, employ the overhead projection to illustrate their lectures.

Opaque Projector. In most forms of still projection light is passed through transparent materials. The opaque projector is used for projecting onto a screen images of non-transparent objects. The opaque projector contains a mirror which reflects light from the object being shown through a lens and onto a screen.

Opaque projectors may be used to project images of book illustrations, flat pictures, drawings, and small objects. Any non-transparent object that can be positioned into the projection area can be imaged on the screen.

Opaque projectors are often bulky, noisy, and cumbersome. The image projected by an opaque projector is not usually as bright as the image projected by the overhead projector. The chief use of the opaque projection is to illustrate lectures.

Audio Recording. In the past several years more and more teachers have turned to the audio tape (usually in cassette form) as an educational tool and technique. One of the greatest temptations for a teacher is to play lengthy (more than ten minutes) audio tapes for learners. In my experience the audio tape does not have the impact on learners that is enjoyed by visual media. Audio tape presentations should be short and sweet.

More lengthy audio tape presentations may be used within the framework of individual methods. Audio tape presentations have been used by teachers and learners to good effect on an individual basis while driving an automobile. On long trips it is possible to listen to the lectures presented at an entire workshop or conference.

Instrumental Techniques: Group Patterns

Techniques are ways of organizing people for learning and putting them into contact with subject matters. When instrumental techniques are employed in groups, they resemble nothing more than the lecture. The attention of the learners is focused on a screen or in the direction of the tape recorder much in the same way their attention is focused on a speaker who is presenting a lecture. The use of the electronic media mentioned above patterns or structures learners in a way that does not promote a high degree of social interaction. While

In my experience the audio tape does not have the impact on learners that is enjoyed by visual media. Audio tape presentations should be short and sweet.

instrumented techniques should not be discounted, teachers should not become so enchanted by techniques employing electronic media that they fail to add other non-instrumental techniques to the repertoire of skills. There has been a tendency during the past several years to bombard learners with images and sounds emitted from electronic media. There is a place for this, of course. But there is also a place for techniques or ways that organize people for more active involvement in the learning process.

Non-Instrumental Techniques

Any number of non-instrumental techniques could be discussed here. For the sake of brevity I shall limit this section of the chapter to a consideration of ten non-instrumental techniques: the lecture, the forum, the panel, the colloquy, the symposium, the buzz session, group discussion, role play, the interview, and the creative action group.

Lecture. The lecture technique is familiar to everyone. A person possessing some expertise in a particular area delivers an oral presentation to an audience. The lecture may be declarative (imparting information), inquiry-oriented (raising questions for the audience to deal with after the lecture), exhortatory (calling forth a sense of commitment or feeling from the audience), or expository (clarifying the implications of an issue).

The members of the audience are asked to participate by listening to the lecturer. While listening is a form of participation, it is not a form that requires ostensible activity from the learners. The flow of communication is ordinarily uni-directional.

Lecture

Forum. The forum technique may be used by groups ranging in approximate size from 20 to 30. Under the direction of a moderator, the audience carries on an open discussion with a resource person or resource persons. While members of the

audience **may** ask questions of the resource persons, members
of the audience may also evaluate the comments of the
resource persons, offer information, and contribute in any way
to the clarification of an issue. The moderator functions to
recognize persons in the audience so they may speak.

Forum

xxx   (resource persons)

x (moderator)

xxxxxxxxxx

xxxxxxxxxx

xxxxxxxxxx

Panel. The panel consists of three to five persons who carry
on a discussion in front of an audience. The moderator functions to recognize persons in the panel so they may speak.
Sometimes use is made of the expanding panel after the panel
discussion has carried on for 30 minutes or so.

Panel

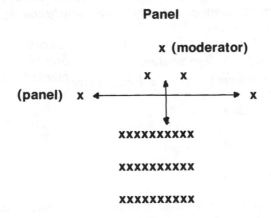

x (moderator)

x   x

(panel) x   x

xxxxxxxxxx

xxxxxxxxxx

xxxxxxxxxx

Expanded Panel

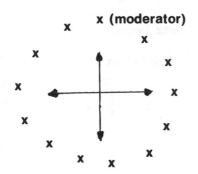

x (moderator)

As is evidenced in the diagram, the expanded panel consists simply of a large circle. The panel members who have previously discussed an issue are joined by the members of the audience for an open discussion under the direction of the moderator.

Colloquy. The colloquy is somewhat akin to the panel. Under the guidance of a moderator resource persons discuss an issue with representatives from the audience.

Colloquy

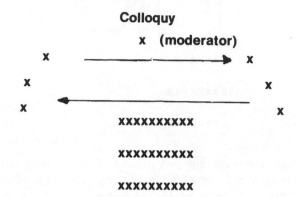

Symposium. A symposium is a series of speeches addressed to different aspects of a topic or related topics. In a symposium the speakers do not address one another; remarks are addressed to the audience. Usually there are three to five speakers in a symposium.

Symposium

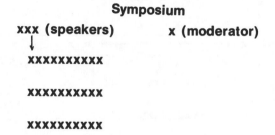

Buzz session. In a buzz session members of the audience are asked to divide into small groups (5-7 members) for the purpose of briefly discussing an issue. After the buzz groups have discussed an issue for about ten minutes, a recorder from each group ordinarily presents a summary of the discussion for the entire audience.

Buzz Session

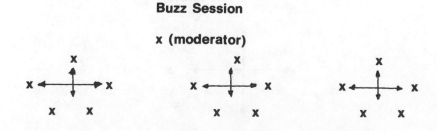

Group discussion. While in one sense group discussion may be considered a method, e.g., the Tuesday night discussion group, group discussion in another sense may be thought of as a technique, e.g., group discussion after a speech at a workshop. The discussion group differs from the buzz group in that the membership of the discussion group is usually 12-15 members and the discussion group meets for a longer period of time (30-60 minutes). A discussion group has a designated leader and a recorder. The recorder usually offers a summary report of the discussion for the entire audience.

Group Discussion

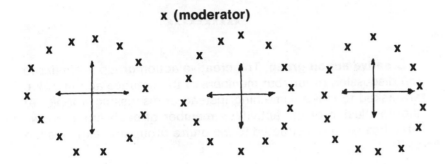

Role play. Role play is acting; it is spontaneous acting. Role players are asked to assume fictitious identities and to react to specific situations. The role play activities are carried out in front of the audience. For example, to dramatize communication difficulties in families three persons are asked to role play this situation: a young high school girl arrives home after a date at a late hour; her parents confront her and discuss her behavior with the girl. One person is asked to play the part of the girl; two other persons are asked to play the parts of the parents.

The role play technique is usually followed by another technique, e.g., the expanded panel, for the purpose of analysing and commenting on what developed during the role play activity.

Role Play

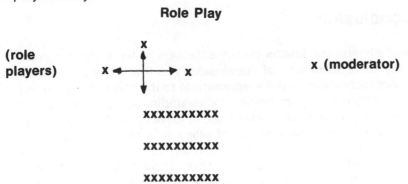

Interview. During the interview a moderator directs a series of planned questions to a respondent or respondents. The respondents know in advance the questions that will be asked. The interview is typically followed by another technique to involve the audience more actively, e.g., forum.

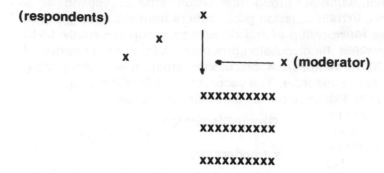

Creative action group. The creative action group is similar to the discussion group, but members of the creative action group are asked to make something instead of discussing a topic. At the conclusion of the activity, a member of each group shows what has been constructed to the entire group and explains the artifact.

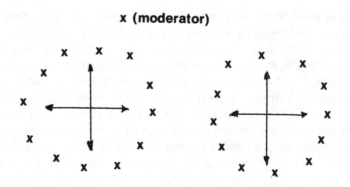

Conclusion

Four general guidelines on the selection of techniques can be recommended by way of conclusion. The first guideline is this: Select techniques that are appropriate to the methods which are used. While it is permissible, for example, to ask a learner to listen to a 60 minute audio tape in directed individual study, such a request would be out of place in a class, a discussion group, or a workshop. Group learning is quite different from individualized learning and this should be taken into consideration when techniques are determined.

Secondly, techniques should be varied from one episode to the next. In a class, for example, the teacher and learners should plan for the use of different techniques to keep the class fresh. Nothing leads to educational stagnation more than the overuse of a particular technique.

Thirdly, techniques are related to content or subject matter. Content, therefore, should be considered in selecting techniques. Some techniques are more effective for transmitting informational data; other techniques are more suitable for encouraging social interchange and communication among the learners.

Fourthly, different combinations of techniques should be used within the context of a particular educational episode. During a given class session the learners may be shown a filmstrip; this may be followed by a panel discussion and an expanded panel. In another situation a lecture may be followed by buzz sessions or creative action groups. A technique, by itself, is seldom productive of much learning. Techniques should be yoked together systematically.

Finally, adult learners themselves may be employed as resource persons in certain areas of study. It is not always necessary, in all content areas, to call in experts to serve as resource persons. At times some of the adult learners can become "experts" in a week's time by reading and studying materials that have been identified by the teacher, and by reading and studying other materials they have selected.

Teaching-learning techniques are extremely important in adult education. In many ways the medium is the message, the process is the product, and the technique is the teaching. How adults learn is just as important as what they learn. For this reason techniques should be determined only after much thought and reflection.

Teaching-learning techniques are extremely important in adult education. In many ways the medium is the message, the process is the product and the technique is the teaching.

142

17. A Fun Technique: Simulation Gaming

In the previous chapter a number of instrumental and non-instrumental techniques were listed and briefly explained. In the category of instrumental techniques some teaching-learning techniques involving the use of electronic media were discussed. In this chapter I wish to treat another type of instrumental technique that is not necessarily an electronic medium: simulation gaming.

A simulation game is a technique which places the learners in a make-believe world, with assumed identities and the requirement that learners make decisions under the constraint of rules. Usually the learner or team of learners making the most realistic decision is declared the winner of the game.

Anyone who has played *Monopoly* is to some extent familiar with simulation gaming, although the educational payoffs of Monopoly are minimal. Again, anyone who has played chess, has been involved in a form of simulation gaming. Using *Monopoly* and chess as examples, the following chart shows some of the elements of a simulation game.

Game Aspect	Monopoly	Chess
Simulated universe	The world of real estate	The military/political world
Scenario: description of the simulated universe	Game instructions and board	Game instructions, board, chess pieces
Roles: identities assumed by players	Monopolists	Strategists
Resources: what is needed to reach goals	Play money, deeds	Chess pieces
Goals	To gain all money and property	To place opposing king in check
Educational objective	(?) understanding of human nature	(?) strategic and tactical thinking

Some Examples

Perhaps there is no better way of illustrating what simulation games are than to describe actual games. In this chapter I shall describe two simulation games: *The Gospel Game* and *Parish*

Finance Game. The former game is unpublished; the latter game has been produced by Twenty-Third Publications.

The purpose of *The Gospel Game* is to help learners become familiar with the main themes of the four gospels.

Every simulation game has a scenario which describes the simulated universe and profiles which describe the roles the players are to assume. In *The Gospel Game* the learners are informed that they are living in the age of the barbarian invasions. The learners are assigned to small groups. Each group represents the surviving Christians of a particular village destroyed by the barbarians.

The barbarians have looted and destroyed everything of value in the villages; they have burned all copies of the New Testament. The surviving Christians in each village take it upon themselves to recall pertinent passages from the gospels and to put these recollections down on paper. Once the remembered gospel fragments have been committed to paper, it will be possible to hand these documents down to the next generation of Christians.

The learners are to play the roles of transmitters of a written record of the gospels; in their groups they will write out a "gospel" from memory of what has been read to them in the past. The teacher may wish to furnish an outline or structure around which the learners will be able to reconstruct a "gospel." This outline may feature the main sections of the real gospels: 1) infancy narratives, 2) the beginning of the public life of Jesus, 3) the sayings of Jesus, 4) the deeds of Jesus, and 5) the resurrection narrative. Working in groups the learners are allowed 45 minutes to reconstruct a "gospel" to pass on to the next generation of Christians.

The winner of the game is decided on the basis of competition among the groups of surviving Christians. The goal for each group is to remember and record as many significant gospel ideas as possible in a 45 minute period. After the 45 minute period, the "gospels" of the groups are exchanged and corrected. The learners of one group correct the "gospel" of another group. During this time they may refer to their bibles. One point is given for each significant detail transcribed in the "gospel" and one point is deducted for each error discovered in the "gospel." The group with the highest number of points is declared winner. The teacher is the court of last resort in settling disputed questions.

Educational Outcomes

Educational outcomes will vary from one group of learners to another. Generally the game assists the learners to focus on the content of the written gospels. It encourages activity on the part of the learners and liberates them from passivity. The learners become more directly involved in the learning process and are required to do more than pay attention to the words of a teacher. Active participation in the learning process is more or less insured when the learners strive for the reward of winning the game.

Further outcomes of *The Gospel Game* may be listed:

1. The learners search their memories and record what they remember in an orderly narrative arrangement. This activity supports the future remembrance of gospel ideas.

2. The learners become aware of what they have remembered of the gospels and what they have forgotten. Subsequent to the playing of the game, a discussion session may be conducted to investigate why they have remembered certain things and forgotten others. Do we remember only what we want to remember? Do people practice forgetfulness when it comes to certain passages in the New Testament? Which passages are most likely to be forgotten? A complete schedule of discussion questions can be designed to follow-up the playing of the game.

3. The written "gospels" prepared by the learners will show the discrepancy between what they recall of the gospels and the gospels themselves. The experience of this discrepancy may be used as a basis for a discussion on how mistakes crept into the written gospels as they were handed down from one generation to the next. The experience may also be employed to show that the written gospels of today are free of substantial error resulting from the transmission process.

4. Learners will be motivated to give close attention to the content of the real gospels when they are busy checking the "gospels" of their fellow learners for errors.

The *Parish Finance Game* was developed by this writer for Twenty-Third Publications. The game is designed for two groups of adult learners. Each of the groups becomes a collective manager of parish finances over a period of four months.

Information about parish income and options for expenditures are printed on a deck of cards. The cards are arranged in order prior to the game and are turned over one-by-one during the game. The two groups, working separately, determine how to spend parish income. This determination is made on the basis of group discussion and consensus. A recorder in each group takes care of the parish ledger; he adds parish income to the amount in the bank and subtracts amounts spent by the group.

At the conclusion of the game the two groups compare their ledgers and discuss what prompted certain expenditures. The winner is decided, by the players, on the basis of how parish money was spent. The group that used money in a prudent, realistic, and Christian manner wins the game.

Educational Outcomes

1. Ideally the players of *Parish Finance Game* will attain some notion of the complex judgments associated with the

financial management of a parish. Although budgetary judgments are simplified for the purposes of the game, a sufficient degree of complexity is involved to permit the players to gain a general insight into the many aspects of management.

2. During the course of the game the players are enabled to identify their values and priorities. In this regard the game could be called a values clarification game. Players will gain understandings of the ways in which they relate to various issues discussed in the game.

3. The game stimulates group discussion of various issues, e.g., parochialism versus universalism, education, ecumenism, etc. Out of the group discussion the players will at least be exposed to different points of view and to new information forthcoming from other members of the group.

The *Parish Finance Game* and *The Gospel Game* may be charted in the same way the games of *Monoploy* and chess were previously outlined.

Game Aspect	Gospel Game	Parish Finance Game
Simulated universe	a Christian community	a local parish
Scenario: description of the simulated universe	the aftermath of a barbarian invasion	a parish confronted with decisions about fiscal affairs
Roles: identities assumed by the players	preservers of the gospels	managers of parish finances
Resources: what is needed to reach goals	memory of the gospels	money, ability to make fiscal decisions
Goals	to reconstruct the essence of the written gospels	to manage a parish in a prudent, realistic, and Christian manner
Educational objectives	various (see above)	various (see above)

Why Use Simulation Gaming?

The best way to learn the educational technology of simulation gaming is to play various simulation games. The description of simulation gaming provided in the foregoing paragraphs, however, should be adequate as an introduction to simulation gaming. What remains now is the consideration of a few questions about adult education vis-a-vis simulation gaming. First of all, why should adult educators employ simulation gaming as a technique?

It cannot be shown that the simulation gaming technique is significantly more effective in transmitting information than traditional instructional techniques. Research on the relative value of simulation gaming versus other techniques is hard to come by. **Some** simulation games are more effective, though, than **some** traditional techniques. A blanket statement about the effectiveness of simulation gaming cannot be made due to the wide differences that exist among various games. Some games are excellent; some are poor. It is very difficult, then, to frame absolute statements about the simulation gaming technique in general.

It can be said with great assurance that use of the simulation gaming technique is highly involving. Learners are taken out of the roles of passive listeners and participate actively in the learning process. Social interchange among the learners is stimulated. The traditional setting of "schooling" is displaced by a new and attractive educational setting.

Another reason may be stated in support of the use of the simulation gaming technique: invariably learners are motivated to take part in the gaming (learning) process. If the game is at all playable, learners will take enjoyment out of the learning process. To my way of thinking this is the strongest reason recommending the use of simulation gaming in adult education. When people can learn and have fun simultaneously, the educational technique that encourages this should at least be seriously considered for use.

Appropriate for Adults?

It is sometimes objected that simulation games are more appropriate for children than for adults—an objection that assumes adults do not delight in play. If Huizinga[1] is correct in defining man as **homo ludens**—playing man—it would seem that the capacity for play is lifelong and that adults no less than children would be attracted to simulation gaming as a technique for learning.

Bischoff[2] accounts for several factors that explain the value of play for middle-aged adults: the need to expend surplus energy, the need for relaxation, the need for an outlet for emotional tensions, and the need to identify and construct other personality patterns for themselves by means of self-expression. After exhaustive research in this area I have not turned up any

If Huizinga is correct in defining man as *homo ludens*—playing man—it would seem that the capacity for play is lifelong and that adults no less than children would be attracted to simulation gaming as a technique for learning.

[1] Huizinga, Johann, *Homo Ludens: A Study of the Play Element in Culture,* Boston: Beacon Press, 1955.

[2] Bischoff, L., *Adult Psychology,* New York: Harper and Row, 1969, p. 173.

data which supports the contention that simulation games are more congenial for childhood learning. The assumption that simulation gaming is the restricted preserve of children is a gratuitous assumption.

It is a significant historical fact, by the way, that the origin of early simulation games was related to a need for an effective technology for adult education and training. In the modern era complex simulation games came into being as early as 1798 with the creation of *Neue Kriegspiel* by the German general staff. Games that simulated war and battle conditions became popular in the military academies of several nations.[3] In the latter 1950's business and industry, given impetus by the American Management Association, began to develop simulation games for management training.[4] While simulation games are used frequently in childhood education, the historic roots of simulation gaming for education reach deeply into the roots of adult education.

Game Design

A number of simulation games are available on the commercial market. Relatively few simulation games, however, have been developed specifically for adult religious education. This situation sometimes challenges teachers of adults to invent and design their own games.

Anyone who has played a few simulation games, and is somewhat imaginative, can design simulation games to meet particular educational needs. Procedural models for game design abound. Two of the most promising design models are the Horn[5] and the Abt[6] model. Each of these models suggests the steps a person must take to design a simulation game.

Many teachers of adults will doubtlessly shy away from designing games fearing that too much work is required. I have discovered—in a course I teach on the design of games—that

[3]Raser, J.R., *Simulation and Society,* Boston: Allyn & Bacon, Inc., 1969, p. 3.

[4]Taylor, John, and Walford, Rex, *Simulation in the Classroom,* Penguin Books, Baltimore: 1972, p. 23.

[5]Zuckermann, D.W. and Horn, R.E., *The Guide to Simulations/Games for Education and Training,* Information Resources, Lexington, Massachusetts, 1973.

[6]Glazier, R., *How to Design Educational Games,* Abt Associates, Cambridge, Massachusetts, 1969.

people generally are filled with ideas for games after they have played several games, and that while time and effort are certainly necessary to move through the design process, the design process itself is much fun.

Conclusion

It must not be inferred from this brief chapter that simulation gaming represents a universal anodyne for all educational ills. An instructional tool—including simulation games—is only as effective as the teacher who employs the tool. Simulation gaming technology will not revolutionize adult religious education, but this technology can go a long way in improving the quality of adult learning. Simulation gaming, then, should be seen more as a promise than a panacea.

THE PARISH FINANCE GAME

. . . to find out what your real priorities are!

by Leon McKenzie

How to Play

THE PARISH FINANCE GAME is designed for two groups of from 3 to 6 players each. (This 8-page section has the material for one group.) The two groups should be situated in different parts of the room and must not communicate with each other during the playing of the game.

After the groups have completed the game, participants should form one discussion group and compare game outcomes.

Following the comparison of outcomes, the discussion questions on the last page are to be considered. IMPORTANT: DO NOT REFER TO DISCUSSION SHEET UNTIL THE END.

PLAYING THE GAME

Each group of players represents a collective manager of a parish. The purpose of the players is to conduct the parish as best they are able.

Detach the 80 cards on the following pages and arrange them face down from 1 to 80. A stack of cards is to be placed before the players in each group in numerical sequence.

Players should take turns drawing the cards singly and reading each card aloud.

Some of the cards will indicate income and some will show expenses; other cards will call for a decision to spend money from the Balance on Hand. The players should reach a consensus judgment when a decision is required. (It is understood that not all information is given to reach a truly wise decision; the decisions have purposely been left "open.")

Income is added to the Balance on Hand on The Parish Ledger sheet. Expenses and outlay of money are subtracted from the Balance on Hand. (Page 6). Itemize all income and expenditures (Page 6).

Once you have finished with a card, you may not return to it later.

Once a decision has been made, you must stick to that decision unless presented with an option to change.

Your parish will begin the game with $6000 as a Balance on Hand.

Begin by drawing card 1. (Income from card 1 has already been tabulated on The Parish Ledger sheet to show the procedure you are to follow. Add or subtract amounts from Balance on Hand immediately and do not wait until the end of the month to show gain or loss. You should know the precise Balance on Hand before you draw each card).

1st Sunday in May Collection: $1635 Add to Balance on Hand	A former parishioner has died. He bequeathed $1900 to the parish. Add $1900 to Balance on Hand	Set this card aside. It may come in handy later. This card entitles you to borrow up to $5000 from a local bank. You may borrow at any time. If you borrow anything and wait until the end of the game to repay the loan, you must pay an interest rate of 10%. If you borrow anything and pay off the debt before the end of the game, you must pay an interest rate of 5%.	Rectory salaries and food allowance: $975 Subtract this from Balance on Hand.
alaries (Rectory): astor..............................$250 ssociate ....225 ousekeeper ....200 ood ....300 ubtract $975 from Balance on and	The pamphlet rack at the rear of the church lost money again this month. Pay $27 and subtract this from Balance on Hand. Do you wish to keep the rack? It is a losing proposition moneywise. Decide.	4th Sunday in May Collection: $1327 Add to Balance on Hand.	School Salaries: $4000 Subtract from Balance on Hand.
alaries (School): Sisters.............................$400 Lay Teachers...................$3200 Janitor...............................400 ubtract $4000 from Balance on and	3rd Sunday in May Collection: $1508 Add to Balance on Hand.	The CCD program has been operating during the year. Students enrolled: 325. The teachers want to take them on a picnic. Will you provide funds for a picnic? How much? If you disburse any money, subtract the amount from Balance on Hand.	It has been suggested that two of the eight grades in the parish school be phased out. This will save you $1600 per month in terms of lay teachers' salaries. Decide what to do.
e Sister Principal of the school quests $180 for instructional aterials. ill you provide the funds? Why? hy not? funds are provided, subtract tal from Balance on Hand	The teachers in the CCD Summer School request the following: $500 for instructional materials 300 for teachers courses 200 for "treats" for the children. There will be 135 children enrolled. How much will you budget for the summer school? Will you grant more than has been requested? Why? Why not? Subtract distribution of funds from Balance on Hand.	The teachers in the parish school have heard of the CCD request for a picnic. They want a picnic for the 172 students in the school. Will you provide the funds? How much? Subtract any disbursement from the Balance on Hand.	If you have already phased out the pamphlet rack, proceed to next card. If you kept the rack, subtract $31 from Balance on Hand.
2nd Sunday in May Collection: $1690 Add to Balance on Hand	Bingo will net you over $400 per month. Do you wish to have Bingo? If you decide to have Bingo in the parish hall you will receive a monthly income from the game. Discuss and decide. Collect nothing now if you wish to have Bingo. You must wait for a few weeks.	Pay utility bill of $192 for the entire parish plant. Subtract $192 from Balance on Hand.	Did you decide to have flowers for the altar? Pay $65 and subtract from Balance on Hand. If you decided against flowers, proceed to next card.
any people are disturbed by ying babies during Mass. A cry om can be provided for $1600. ill you spend the money? Why? hy not? the room is constructed, sub- ct $1600 from Balance on Hand	A florist will supply flowers for the altar at a cost of $65 per month. Do you wish to have flowers for the altar? Why? Why not? If you want flowers, subtract $65 from the Balance on Hand.	The centennial committee of your town's Chamber of Commerce is seeking funds for civic decorations. Will you give anything? Subtract any gift from Balance on Hand.	2nd Sunday in June Collection: $1627 Add to Balance on Hand.
e two Sisters who teach in the arish school are going to attend summer educational workshop. ey need $200 each to help fray expenses. Will you con- bute all, part or none of the 00. Why? Why not? a contribution is made, subtract tal from Balance on Hand	A former member of the parish is now a missionary priest in South America. He asks for a donation from the parish for his mission. Will you give him something? How much? If you give, subtract the amount from Balance on Hand.	1st Sunday in June Collection: $1802 Add to Balance on Hand.	A Jewish orphanage has asked for a donation. It takes $1200 to support one child for one year. Will the parish "adopt" a child? Will you pay something toward the support of a child? How much? Discuss and decide. Subtract any donation from Balance on Hand.

154

22   15   8   1

23   16   9   2

24   17   10   3

25   18   11   4

                  5

26   19   12

27   20   13   6

28   21   14   7

A local Catholic high school asks the parishes to contribute scholarships for needy students. Each scholarship costs $500. Decide what to do. Any disbursement is to be subtracted from Balance on Hand.	Beginning of the fiscal year. Pay insurance for parish plant: $786 Pay Cathedraticum (tax to diocese), $1008 Subtract total from Balance on Hand.	If you have a pamphlet rack, pay $27 and subtract this from Balance on Hand.	A migrant worker was rushed to the hospital and required minor surgery. His hospital bill is $672. Will you pay the bill or part of it? He has no money. Any disbursement is to be subtracted from Balance on Hand.
3rd Sunday in June Collection: $1247 Add to Balance on Hand.	People have noticed that the Mass vestments are somewhat frayed. A new set of vestments will cost $650. Will you buy a new set? Why? Why not? If you purchase the vestments, subtract the amount from Balance on Hand.	Several months ago a piece of parish property was sold. The transaction has been finalized. Add $2000 to Balance on Hand. You may bank any amount now. The funds *must* remain in the bank until the end of the game if you wish to collect 5% interest. No further banking will be permitted during the game. Should you run in the red, continue deficit spending.	If you have Bingo at your parish, collect $478 and add this to Balance on Hand. If you do not have Bingo, proceed to next card.

The local ministerial alliance seeks a contribution to further ecumenical education in your town.
Will you give anything? Why? Why not?
If you contribute, subtract the amount from Balance on Hand.
	If you decided previously to have Bingo, collect $423 and add to Balance on Hand.
	If you decided against Bin proceed to next card.
		2nd Sunday in July
		Collection: $1501
		Add to Balance on Hand.
			4th Sunday in July
			Collections:
			    If you hired fund raisers $1678
			    If you did not hire them ..1307
			    If you decided not to repair the kneelers, subtract $375
			    (People were quite upset).
			You may now pad the worn kneelers if you wish Cost: $587. Subtract this from Balance on Hand if disbursed.

Migrant workers will be living in your parish during July and August. They want to use the parish hall as a child-care center. Will you permit this? Why? Why not? They also ask for $1000 to purchase food and equipment for the center. Will you donate anything? How much? Why? Why not? Subtract any disbursement from Balance on Hand.	A professional fund raising organization wants to increase your Sunday collections by tithing. If you employ the fund raisers, your collections will probably go up. Otherwise they will probably remain the same. The fund raisers ask $1000. Discuss and decide. If you hire the organization, subtract $1000 from Balance on Hand.	If you have flowers for the altar pay $65 and subtract this amount from balance on Hand.	A Protestant church in the neighborhood has burned to the ground. They want to use your church or parish hall. Decide. Will you contribute anything to their building fund? Why? Why not? How much? Subtract any gift disbursement Settle accounts with bank regarding investments or loans. Determine final Balance on Hand.
There has been a flood in a neighboring town. The call has gone out for financial contributions for the homeless. Will you give anything? Why? Why not? How much? If you decide to help, subtract the amount from Balance on Hand.	1st Sunday in July Collection: $1574 Add to Balance on Hand.	Pay utilities: $154 Subtract this from Balance on Hand.	The Society for the Ordination of Women Priests has written a letter asking for a donation to support their cause. Will you contribute anything? Why? Why not? If you contribute, subtract the amount from Balance on Hand.

4th Sunday in June
Collection: $1246
Add to Balance on Hand.
	Rectory Salaries and Food Allowance: $975
	Subtract this amount from Balance on Hand.
		3rd Sunday in July
		Collection: $1497
		Add to Balance on Hand.
		You may now return to cards 20, 28, 29, and 33. Do you wish to give more to these causes? Subtract any amount you give from the Balance on Hand.
			5th Sunday in July
			Collections:
			    If you hired fund raisers $985
			    If you did not hire them 803
			    If you have not as yet padded the kneelers, subtract $175 from your collection. Add the remainder to Balance on Hand.

Utilities bill: $178 Subtract from Balance on Hand.	During the summer months the school janitor works around the parish grounds doing odd jobs. He has no other work. Do you wish to employ him this summer? His salary is $400 per month. Discuss and decide. Subtract any disbursement from Balance on Hand.	The padded kneelers in the church are quite worn. It is distracting to kneel on many of them. Many people have complained. It will cost $587 to repair the worn kneelers. Decide what to do. If you repair the kneelers subtract the amount from Balance on Hand.	A wealthy member of the parish insists strongly that half of the Sunday Masses be in Latin. No one else in the parish has expressed an interest in Latin Masses. Decide what to do. (Remember, he is wealthy).

50

43

36

29

51

44

37

30

52

45

38

31

53

46

39

32

54

47

40

33

55

48

41

34

56

49

42

35

st Sunday in August Collection: If you hired fund raisers $1734 If you did not hire them ..1584 If you have not padded the neelers, subtract $59 from your ollection. If you have not restored atin Masses, subtract $2 from ur collection—the wealthy par-hioner withheld his usual ontribution. Add proper amount Balance on Hand.	If you have a pamphlet rack, pay $34. Subtract this from Balance on Hand.	The local Black Militant Organization wants to use the pulpit next Sunday to talk about racism. Will you permit this? They also seek a donation to support their cause. Will you give anything? Why? Why not? How much? If you contribute, subtract the amount from Balance on Hand.	1st Sunday in September Collection: If you hired fund raisers. 1349 If you did not hire them 1314. A gift from a former parishioner has been received. Add $2000 to your collection. Add total to Balance on Hand.
Rectory Salaries and Food Allow-ance: $975 Subtract this from Balance on Hand.	Some people have noticed that the statues in church need refinishing. If you want them refinished you must pay $550. Decide what to do. Subtract any disbursement from Balance on Hand.	3rd Sunday in August Collection: If you hired fund raisers 1378. If you did not hire them 1242. If you permitted the Black Militants to speak in church, subtract $480 from your collection. The padded kneeler matter has ceased to be an issue.	Rectory Salaries and Food Allow-ance: $975 Subtract this from Balance on Hand.
f you kept the school janitor on uring the summer, pay his salary. ubtract this from Balance on and.($400)	2nd Sunday in August Collection: If you hired fund raisers 1629 If you did not hire them 1498 If you still haven't padded the kneelers, subtract $50 from your collection. Add proper amount to Balance on Hand.	You need a new sound amplification system in the church. Cost: $850. Decide what to do. Any disbursement must be subtracted from Balance on Hand.	School Salaries: If you kept all eight grades.... $4000. If you phased out two grades 2400. Subtract proper amount from Balance on Hand.
tility Bill: $143 ubtract this from Balance on and.	A priest formerly stationed at your parish has left the clerical state and married. He is now in serious financial difficulties. Will you send him anything? Why? Why not? How much? If you send him anything, subtract this from Balance on Hand.	4th Sunday in August Collection: If you hired fund raisers 1237 If you did not hire them 1198. Add proper amount to Balance on Hand.	Pay $147 for utilities. Subtract from Balance on Hand.
If you play Bingo, collect $572 Add this to Balance on Hand.	A local social service agency, nonsectarian and private, is sponsoring a well-baby clinic for the poor. You have been asked to help support the clinic. Will you give anything? How much? Subtract any disbursement from Balance on Hand.	A neighboring Catholic parish is on the verge of bankruptcy. Will you help them by donating money? Why? Why not? If you give anything, subtract this amount from Balance on Hand.	The CCD teachers request the following to get ready for the school year: $2000 for books and materials 500 for filmstrips 200 for incidental expenses Subtract disbursement from Balance on Hand.
f you have flowers for the altar, ay $65. ubtract this from Balance on and.	The heat and humidity in the church for Sunday Mass is really terrific. Many people get sick during Mass. Some older persons have stopped coming because they feel faint in church. For $1800 the air-conditioner can be improved. Will you pay for this? Why? Why not? Subtract any disbursement from Balance on Hand.	Time to get the convent ready for the return of the Sisters. Cost: $178 Subtract from Balance on Hand.	If you are buying flowers for the altar pay $65 and subtract this from Balance on Hand. If you have borrowed money from the bank pay it back with interest and subtract amount from Balance on Hand. If you have banked money, collect it with the added interest. Total up your final account.

Cut apart the cards and arrange them in numeric sequence (from 1 to 80) face-down, so that number 1 is the first drawn.

Please keep in mind that these do not provide all information for the best possible decision; they have been left "open" to stimulate reflection and discussion.

THE PARISH LEDGER

BALANCE ON HAND	ITEM
$ 6000	
+ 1635	Card 1—Sunday Collection
$ 7635	

When this sheet of paper is full, use any other lined sheets to continue. Bring your Balance on Hand forward to the next sheet.

Discussion Questions

(These are to be considered only after the players of the two groups have compared outcomes).

Three major mistakes should have been avoided in the game:

1) The accumulation of a large Balance on Hand. The Church does not exist to make money.

2) The excessive expenditure of money to support the internal structure of the parish with a resultant failure to meet the needs of people outside of the parish.

3) The excessive expenditure of money to meet the needs of people outside of the parish with the resultant financial collapse of the parish structure. A bankrupt parish cannot serve the poor on an ongoing basis.

QUESTION: Which of the two groups, in your opinion, was more successful in avoiding these three mistakes? Discuss.

QUESTION: Compare the funds spent on the maintenance of the parish to the funds spent on charitable works. Which group showed the more realistic ratio? Discuss.

QUESTION: Compare the funds spent on the parish school and the CCD (Pre-school through Adult) programs. Which group showed the more realistic ratio? Discuss.

QUESTION: Compare the funds spent on Catholic projects with the funds spent on Protestant or secular projects? In your opinion, which group showed the more Christian ratio? Discuss.

QUESTION: Did the experience of playing *The Parish Finance Game* teach you anything? What? Discuss.

CONCLUDING NOTE: The amount of money in the Balance on Hand at the conclusion of the game does not determine the winning group.

The winner of the game is the group which used money in a prudent, realistic and Christian manner. Decide which group won.